'What makes Africa poor despite the profusion of natural resources and energetic labour force remains a conundrum. This book attempts to unravel this apparent riddle. It is an important contribution to understanding contemporary African economic realities. This book has been written in a manner that is largely accessible to both academic and non-academic audiences. I recommend the book to all those interested in updating and broadening their understanding about poverty in the 21st century.'

PROF. KITILA MKUMBO, MINISTER OF INDUSTRY AND TRADE, UNITED REPUBLIC OF TANZANIA

'It is now 75 years since Frederick Hayek wrote *The Road Serfdom*. In what could actually be a fitting anniversary follow-up, Erastus Mtui offers us a good sense for where the journey to prolonged poverty originates – within us. In ten chapters – laden with facts and figures – that avoid the pitfalls of the gobbledygook brickbats of academic and professional economists, Mtui focuses on education and a mindset shift among other prescriptions, if Africa is to be liberated, for we are often our worst enemies. His book is, therefore, a worthwhile read for policy-makers and for citizens desirous of escap what I have called the "complicit middle".'

PROF. PATRICK UTOMI, POLITICAL ECONOMIST AND FO NIGERIAN PRESIDENTIAL CANDIDATE

'For a continent that is so rich and yet poverty is so pre this book offers a fresh perspective, poses profound qu and suggests possible solutions that all Africans need t consider carefully and implement. I would recommen book to every young person and every leader in Afric

HARDY PEMHIWA, GROUP CEO, ECONET GROUP, JOHANNESBURG, SOUTH AFRICA

'This book stirs up critical conversations that we must engage in to understand where we find ourselves today, as Africans and to strategise on the path we must chart to secure our future. It is a call to individual and collective action. The future is own hands. It is an important read.'

Edem Senanu, Senior Management and Development Consultant, Accra, Ghana

'The book challenges us with the African future of now. It is that which we ought to have and engage in for the continent's sustainable development. It is a good read for leaders, technocrats and young people to stimulate the necessary discussion for the continent.'

Getrude Mongella, the first Speaker of the Pan-African Parliament

'Mr Mtui has nailed it well. It is all within us. The continent has made great progress but more is demanded from us. These are the conversation that cannot be avoided for the continent to make progress. Thought-provoking book.'

Abdirashid A. Hussein, Conflict Analyst, Development and Peace Building Practioner, Nairobi, Kenya

'Neglected tropical diseases are rooted in – and keep people locked into – cycles of poverty. In the words of Bill Foege, "The slavery of today is poverty", and this book is a powerful reminder that unless we address its root causes, there can be no prosperity. A great and bracing read, with important lessons for us all.'

Dr. Mwele Malecela, Director, Neglected Tropical Diseases, WHO, Geneva, Switzerland. Also named as one of the 100 Most Influential African Women 2021 by Avance Media.

Poverty Within Not on the Skin

First published by Erastus Mtui in 2021

emtui@prasperascons.com

ISBN: 978-9976-5065-1-8

Prepared for print by Staging Post
Cover design by Sam van Straaten
Set in Adobe Caslon Pro 10/14pt
Job no. 003846

Poverty Within Not on the Skin

10 vicious cycles that have kept the African continent in poverty

Erastus Mtui

We can only go as far as what is within us

To my lovely family: my dear wife Violeth and our children, Praise, Priela and Privela. I love you all.

Contents

Acknowledgements

I AGREE WITH BRITISH philosopher James Allen who once said, 'No duty is more urgent than that of returning thanks.'

I am grateful to the Almighty God above all for the health, motivation and faith that kept me going all the time and especially during the Covid-19 pandemic to bring this book to its finality.

I also owe immense thanks to many people who contributed to bring this book to a completion.

First and foremost, to my dearest wife Violeth and our children Praise, Priela and Privela for their unceasing encouragements and support during the writing journey. This is your book and I am forever proud of and grateful for you.

I would like to extend my very special thanks to seasoned and highly respected leaders whose endorsements have enlightened and stirred up the book. I am grateful to Prof. Kitila Mkumbo, the Minister of Industry and Trade of the United Republic of Tanzania; Prof. Patrick Utomi, a political economy and management expert and a former presidential candidate in Nigeria; Dr Peter Mathuki, the secretary general of the East African Community; Getrude Mongela, the first Speaker of the Pan-African Parliament and Secretary-General of the Fourth UN World Conference on Women in Beijing, China; Mr Hardy Pemhiwa, Econet Group CEO; Dr. Mwele Malecela, Director of Neglected Tropical Diseases, World Health Organization-WHO; Mr Edem Senanu, a management and development expert, and Abdirashid A. Hussein, Conflict Analyst, Development and Peace Building Practioner, for their words of wisdom on the book. I am deeply honoured.

My sincere thanks go to the great minds that spent time to review the book and/or supported me in the whole process to get the book to its final piece: Prof. Joseph Semboja, Ambassador Lt. General (Rtd) Paul Ignace Mella, Ambassador Togolani Mavula, Jenerali Ulimwengu, Dr Azaveri Lwaitama, Mr Hank Musolf, Mr Gilbert Mboya, Dr Chris Mauki, Dr Robert Otsina, Mr Clement Ogojgi and Mr John Wise.

The Jacana Media team lead by Aimee Armstrong and Laurianne Claase just to mention a few; you were an incredible team to work with. I am grateful to you all for your editorial and design commitment.

I may not be able to mention everyone who made this book possible, but I am deeply indebted to you all for your immense support and encouragements throughout the scribbling journey.

Thank you all.

Introduction

The African continent has been at the centre of a number of complex and contrary conversations around the globe. Some people depict the African continent negatively, while others praise and admire it. Stories of perseverance and triumph vie with tales of misery, hopelessness and widespread human suffering. The beauty of Africa's natural attractions, its mountains, valleys and wild animals, and its rich history, contrast with heartbreaking stories about deep poverty, never-ending conflicts, poaching and the plundering of the continent's rich resources.

Africa is home to a third of the planet's mineral resources, 12% of global oil reserves, 40% of the world's gold, and close to 90% of the world's platinum[1] with 80% of it in South Africa alone.[2] Platinum is a metal used in electric cars and the electronics industry including the manufacture of computers and mobile phones. Africa also stands out as continent rich in culture. It is estimated that there are 3,000 ethnic groups or nationalities, derogatively called tribes, and more than 2,100 languages[3] on the continent, each ethnic group with its own customs and lifestyles. Yet, despite such diversity, they all have much in common, including ways of living, behaviours and more that hold the continent back and contribute to the continent experiencing a vicious cycle of poverty. Indignation and irritation erupt when non-Africans denigrate the continent using, at times, the same actual behaviours and ways of life of its people that cause poverty. However, ironically, many discussions within Africa echo the same sentiments that anger Africans when voiced by others. These are vibrant and loud conversations.

Then, there are muted discussions that suggest that something is wrong somewhere with many of us Africans. Whether it is an article, or a book written by fellow Africans, or written by 'imperialists', 'colonisers' or 'Westerners' – as many would have it – the discourse is sensitive, heart-rending and usually interpreted differently among societal groups. There are those who have gone so far as to call Africa a 'Dark Continent', while some painfully link the problems on the continent to its indigenous black inhabitants.

There are articles in social media featuring racist writings or utterances purportedly by the apartheid-era former South African prime minister P.W Botha or by former U.S president Donald Trump or, more recently, by the Chinese President Xi Jinping. Whether one considers those articles to be illustrations of fake news or not, they tend to generate fierce discussion and reflection and, to some extent, produce repugnance and anger. Whether the articles are authentic or not, the behaviours, values and cultural practices of many Africans they highlight serve to inflame the debate as to whether such activities if practised by other races would produce the same results. The answer to this conundrum would help address the question of whether it is the colour of skin that causes desolation or what is within.

Africa has been a topic of discussion inside and outside the continent. Unfortunately, it has been most often described, not as a shining North Star, but a lame duck, backward and a dark continent despite the recent, exciting narrative of 'Africa Rising'. The 'Africa Rising' narrative emerged in the late 1990s and early 2000s with coverage by one of the global major tabloids, *Time* (1998) titled, 'Africa Rising: After decades of famine and war, life is finally looking up for many Africans. Here is why'. The excitement and conversations on Africa rising lightened up and blossomed further around 2010s. This time it was the cover story on the front pages of the famous London-based magazine *The Economist* (2011) and the New York-based magazine *Time* (2012). The narrative was based on the good economic growth witnessed in many African countries, backed up by expanding democratisation as well as the increased availability of the internet through mobile phones, growth of entrepreneurship, improvements in the business environment and a rise in consumer spending. While there is nothing wrong with the dubbed titles, they give perspective of what the past has been despite hopes that lie ahead.

According to the World Bank,[4] the continent's economies grew at an average rate of 5–6% between 2004 and 2014. This was, without a doubt, an impressive performance after the very slow growth rate of around 2% in the 1980s and 1990s. However, it is important to note that between 2015 and 2019, the continent only grew by an average of 2.5%, behind the growth rate of the continent's population, which is explored in details in the next chapters.

Several professional, public and business meetings between 2010 and 2020 amplified the 'Africa Rising' excitement, with participants enthusiastically pointing out that six or seven of the ten fastest growing economies in the world were in Africa.[5] McKinsey released a report in 2010 titled, 'Lions on the Move', which predicted great growth for the continent. There was excitement everywhere. Excitement generates a positive drive and motivation, which in turn creates momentum, which is a strong driving force in an economy or businesses when well capitalised. The question is whether Africa should celebrate an average growth of 2.5%. Hard questions need to be asked about the fundamentals needed to boost this growth.

There are many arguments against the 'Africa Rising' narrative. Apart from the modest average economic growth, there are some voices that cite ongoing conflicts in some African countries, a deteriorating business environment in others and very slow growth in Africa's biggest economies like South Africa and Nigeria.[6] The continent, while rich in resources, many of its inhabitants are still poor in most aspects and measures. When it comes to gross domestic product (GDP) per capita, health and education systems, infrastructure and life expectancy, the continent remains far behind.

Education

According to UNESCO,[7] Africa has the highest rates of education exclusion. 'Over one-fifth of children between the ages of about 6 and 11 are out of school' in Sub-Saharan Africa. A region of 46 countries out of the 54 African countries with a total population of 1.1 billion[8] which have 20% of the children between the ages of six and 11 out of school! This rate of education exclusion is very scary. The UNESCO Institute for Statistics[9] says that '...almost 60% of youth between the ages of about 15 and 17...' in the region are also not in school. These are young people who ought to be in middle and higher secondary schools. It is alarming that six out of 10 young people who are supposed to be in school are not. How do we shape a sustainable progressive conversation with such facts? We will dig deeper on this topic in the coming chapters.

FOOD SECURITY

About 70% of continent's population make a living through agriculture[10] which is a significant number for one sector. Surprisingly, even with such a high number of the population involved in agriculture, the continent leads globally in malnutrition and death related to malnutrition. UNICEF (2019)[11] shows that the number of stunted children (a form of malnutrition) increased in every region of Africa, while the same had fallen by 25% worldwide between 2000 and 2019. Something must be very wrong somewhere. One would expect the continent, which largely depends on agriculture to be food secure and self-sufficient, and its people in good health. This is not the case in Africa.

Again, according to a 2019 joint report[12] by UNICEF, WHO and the World Bank Group, Africa is the only continent in the world with a rising number of stunted children, who are significantly shorter for their age than the average, due to malnutrition. The report shows that in Asia, Latin America and the Caribbean, the number of stunted children almost halved between 2000 and 2018. In Africa, for the same reporting period, the number of stunted children increased, as Dr Adesina, president of the African Development Bank, pointed out at a high-level dinner for the African Leaders for Nutrition Initiative in Ethiopia in February 2020. 'Africa is the only continent where the number of stunted children has increased over the last two decades.'[13]

POVERTY

The World Bank report on Africa titled, *Accelerating Poverty Reduction in Africa,* published in October 2019, summarises part of its observations in a heartbreaking sentence: 'The poverty rate in Africa has gone down, but the number of people living in poverty has increased, and global poverty will increasingly become African.'[14] According to the report, by 2030, Africa will be home to 90% of the world's poor. Such a projection is both heartbreaking and tinged with a sense of anger. How would one feel if someone tells him or her that his or her family/clan will make 90% of his or her village's or ward's poverty in ten years' time? However, these are not made-up numbers and assumptions. They are well informed projections and if nothing significant is done about it, reality will come home.

To make more sense about it, in 2015, people who lived in Africa constituted 55% of people who were poor globally. The above projection indicates that Africa will constitute 90% of the world's poverty by 2030. This means it is either poverty is drastically increasing in Africa, or other poor regions in the world are reducing poverty while Africa is stagnant. What is wrong with Africa?

A World Economic Forum article,[15] published in March 2019, indicates that, out of the world's 28 poorest countries, 23 are in Africa. This is sad. Not that it would be better if all 28 countries were from a different continent because every human being should progress and come out of poverty. It is high time to soul search and ask ourselves whether all countries in the continent have actionable plans and deadlines to escape poverty. No wonder the World Bank forecasts that, by 2030, global poverty will be largely African. In other words, without concrete plans and actions to avoid such an outcome, Africa will be the definition of poverty.

It is no wonder that so many young African men and women embark on dangerous journeys in small boats, without lifejackets, to cross the Mediterranean Sea in the hope of finding a better life in Europe. These young people work hard to pay up to US$2,000 to the smugglers who transport them to Europe. We have also witnessed many young people being caught inside containers, sometimes mixed up dangerously with heavy consignments and without enough air, running away from their countries to better economies. A return air ticket from most parts of Africa to Europe is less than US$2,000. However, these young people save to pay these amounts in hope of a better future on the other side of the ocean. These young people could do a lot with US$2,000 in Africa, but the mere promise of a better life in Europe is sufficient enticement to brave the perilous sea crossing. They clearly have despaired and do not see any promise in Africa. We may disagree with this conclusion, but their perspectives drive their actions.

There is no argument about Africa being the poorest continent in the world. We largely complain that Africa has been badly branded around the world by the 'imperialists' just to tarnish our image, but we do little to change the status quo that has prevailed since the dawn of Africa's post colonial era.

Economic progress

In 2019, the continent's GDP was US$2.5 trillion,[16] which was roughly equal to China's GDP in 2005. However, by 2017, which is 12 years from 2005, the World Bank estimated China's GDP to be US$12.2 trillion, an increase of almost 600% over the period. This means the Chinese economy doubled every five years. Could African countries double their economies in five years or even in a decade? Some would say, 'Why not?' Some would say, 'No way' while others would say, 'It depends'. However, with the current trend, it is nearly impossible for the continent to double its economies, even within a 10-year time frame. Even with Africa's resources and capabilities, there are fundamental issues that need to be addressed before that happens.

If we are to see significant changes in Africa, at least 75% of

African economies need to grow in double digits.

The 'Africa Rising' excitement has been celebrated when only 15 of the continent's 54 economies were growing above 5% but below 10%. This is but less than a third of Africa's countries. According to the International Monetary Fund's (IMF) 2019 projections, the four largest countries in Africa by GDP (Nigeria, South Africa, Egypt and Algeria) made up about 53% of the continent's GDP. That means the other 50 countries shared the remaining 47% of the continent's economy.

According to the World Bank, the Sub-Saharan African region combined was estimated to have grown by 2.3% in 2019.[17] The same report showed that this part of the continent had grown below 3% since 2015. To make sense of things, China's economy has been growing at least at a rate of 6% for the last 25 years, which is more than double the current growth rates of the African continent, with the highest growth rate of 14.2% in 1992 and 2007. According to the same World Bank updates, China grew at an average rate of 11.4% for 10 years between 2000 and 2010. The same updates showed that China grew at an average rate of 7.4% between 2011 and 2019, which is a consistent, impressive performance.

It is not enough to compare the percentage growth without looking at the economic bases. For example, an economy with a GDP of US$20 billion, growing at 10%, is not equal to an economy with a GDP of US$1 trillion, growing at 10%. If both economies grew at 10%, the former economy would have added only US$2 billion to its GDP while the latter would have added US$100 billion to its economy, 50 times more than the former.

The continent's economy grew negatively by 2.1% in 2020, as a result of Covid-19 pandemic.[18] On the other hand, in 2019 the continent's economy increased by 3.4% on an estimated GDP base of US$2.5 trillion.[19] This means Africa added only

US$85 billion to its GDP in 2019. On the other hand, China, a single country, which was estimated to have a GDP of US$14.3 trillion in 2019, grew at a rate of 6.1%,[20] adding approximately US$880 billion to its economy in that same year; that is 10 times more than Africa's 54 countries combined.

It is generally expected that a small, developing economy will grow faster than a developed economy because of more opportunities. However, this is not the case for many African countries. Sub-Saharan Africa combined grew at a rate of less than 3% for five consecutive years to 2020 and less than 5% for 10 years to 2020. Unfortunately, because of the modest size of their economies, single-digit growth rates cannot transform African countries quickly enough. There is nothing to celebrate in average growth rates of around 3%. How is Africa ever going to catch up with developed countries when the whole continent's growth contributes far less than US$100 billion annually, while a single developed country contributes 10 times as much? We cannot benchmark our performance against each other. All too often, we compare ourselves with countries that are not doing as well as us, and derive from this a false sense of confidence, achievement and probably contentment. African countries should not be satisfied by higher or faster growth relative to each other. The questions should be, what is each country's road-map, and how fast is the country going to lift its people from poverty?

Gross Domestic Product/Growth rates: Other countries

Given its low level of development, the continent should have blossomed with higher growths. This does not refer to its immensely rich resources as the driver, but, by virtue of having a low base, the general rule is that it should be growing faster than developed economies.

There are several countries that do not have Africa's resources, but are, nevertheless, highly developed. In the early 1960s, for example, Singapore was at the same level of development as many African countries. Singapore's GDP per capita was US$428 but has since then grown to US$65,233 in 2019.[21] Comparatively, the same report shows the Sub-Saharan Africa's GDP per capita was US$131.6 in 1960 and has grown to only US$1,596 in 2019.These are two worlds' apart comparisons.

According to the same World Bank updates,[22] the GDP of the United States of America in 2019 was US$21.4 trillion, having grown from US$19.519 trillion in 2017, adding almost US$2 trillion over two years, which is not too far from the entire African continent economies. In other words, growing at the same rate, in just two years the United States' economy could produce wealth almost equivalent to the entire African economy.

Within the United States, the State of California alone had a GDP of US$3.2 trillion in 2019, up 3.4% (2019), which is more than Africa's entire continental economy. California has a bigger economy and grew faster than the 46 Sub-Saharan African countries in 2019. One may be tempted to explain these development gaps by pointing out that the United States of America got independence more than 200 years ago and China was never colonised, and therefore cannot be compared to any African nation.

In less than 30 years, between 1981 and 2008, China lifted some 600 million people out of extreme poverty. China's per capita income increased fivefold from just over US$300 in 1990 to roughly US$1,000 in 2000, and it increased again fivefold from US$1,000 in 2000 to US$4,500 in 2010, and to more than US$10,000 in 2019 despite the size of its population. In just 20 years, China's per capita income increased 25-fold. The fact that China was never colonised is irrelevant, as over this 20-year period, all African countries were already independent.

The aim here is not to discuss China or to compare it with the United States, but rather to contemplate Africa's fundamentals and deliberate on what it is that is holding it back and what will and what will not help it kickstart the continent's development.

In 2009, the three largest economies in the world were the USA (US$14.1 trillion), Japan (US$5.1 trillion) and China (US$4.9 trillion). Japan remained in second position for several years. For China to overtake Japan and close in on the United States, it had to grow much faster. In 2019, the Chinese GDP reached US$14.3 trillion, while the United States of America was worth US$21.43 trillion. Japan's GDP for 2019 came in (stagnated) at US$5.1 trillion.[23]

As it is evident, both the Chinese and North American economies have been growing since 2009. The difference is the growth rates. If China had been growing at the same rate as the USA, then the gap between China and the USA would have been much bigger. In 2009, the United States economy was more than three times that of China. However, 10 years later – or two presidential terms for most African countries – China had significantly closed the gap. In just 10 years, China almost tripled its economy, despite the fact that its population was relatively poorer than that of the US or Japan. China has blossomed in the last 20 years. This is equivalent to two two-term presidents in Africa for a country like Tanzania, which has a maximum of two five- year presidential terms. In the year 2000, China's GDP was only US$1.2 trillion, shooting to US$14.3 trillion in 2019, which is an increase of almost 12 times in 20 years. This is a world record success and is partly explained by the poverty alleviation programmes that were put in place.

According to *The Economic Times* magazine,[24] China lifted 68 million people out of poverty in five years between 2012/13 and 2017/18, more than 1 million people a month.

Such outcomes boosted the economy, helping China to grow even faster.

Let the focus of of this discussion shift from China to Africa. Africa remains behind the curve and it is not catching up with the rest of the world. Below is an IMF factual chat showing the increasing gap between Sub-Saharan Africa and the rest of the world.

Figure I.1: A growing income gap

The income gap between Sub-Saharan Africa and the rest of the world, based on real GDP per capita, grows wider. (Index 2019 =100)[25]

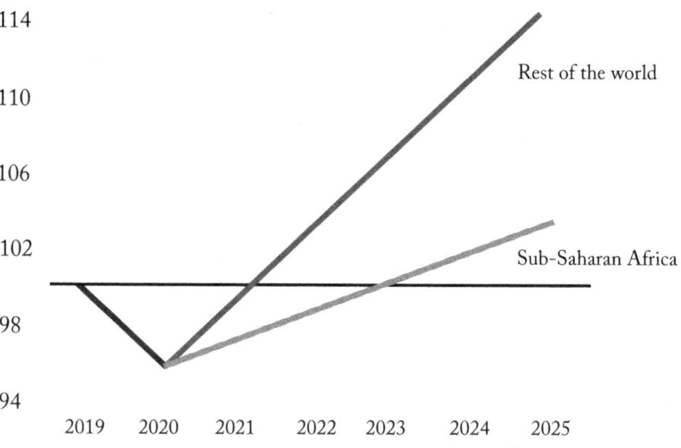

Sources: IMF Staff Calculations, World Economic Outlook database

Unfortunately, the above graph shows how Africa will be left behind even further if we don't get our act together. This does not mean the continent will not be making progress, no! However,other countries will be doing better. One may say that they have better human capital and technology, but how much is Africa doing to close the gap? That is a very heavy question.

This graph should provoke serious reflections and actions from all angles of the African continent, governments, market places, regional economic blocs and among individual Africans. Africa cannot sit comfortably with these projected realities to materialise. We cannot be a continent that blames everyone else except ourselves.

Employment

Africa's economic growth has not generated enough jobs. According to *African Report* magazine,[26] overall employment on the continent grew by only 2.8% between 2000 and 2008 while overall economic growth was roughly twice as much. This means economies grew, but that growth did not translate to job creation. This has been an ongoing scenario on the continent even for the years after 2008, up until 2014. This means African economies are not growing for the majority, but are, rather, growing for the few. The small increases in absolute economic contribution are insufficient to fund much-needed infrastructure or healthcare systems for a burgeoning population. This is the genesis of the vicious cycle of poverty, in which poverty begets poverty and traps people in poverty.

This concept, 'the vicious cycle of poverty' is at the centre of deliberations in this book. One of the simplest definitions of the term states that the vicious cycle of poverty is 'an illustration on how poverty begets poverty, and how poverty itself traps the poor into staying in poverty'.[27]

According to Professor Nurkse, an Estonian economist, the vicious cycle of poverty is caused by a lack of capital formation, which, in turn, is mainly caused by low income. Because of low production, one cannot save money to use as a capital; low capital leads to low investment, which, in turn, leads to low production and low income. Thus, the cycle continues.

The aim of the book is not to wade through theoretical

definition of the terminology but rather reflect on how webbed the continent issues are and whether there is a plausible way out.

This book recounts different issues, challenges, conditions and mainly ways of life that entrench poverty and continued to 'guarantee' poverty in the continent.

To change this trajectory, the foundations and structures of the continent's economy must be reformed.

Figure I.2: The vicious cycle of poverty

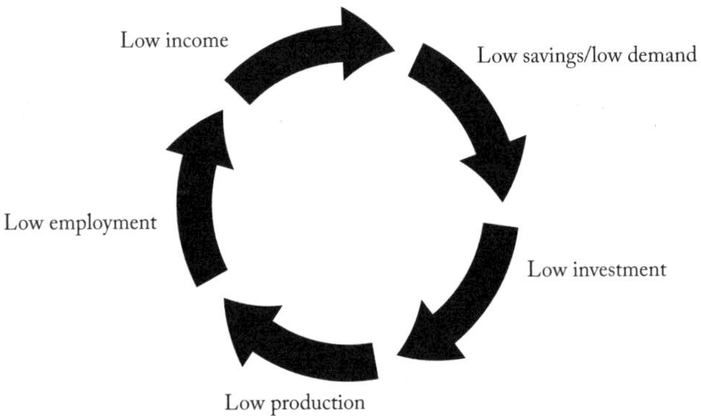

Source: Author's own based on Nurkse's propagation

This book is intended as a soul-searching exercise and an analysis of fundamental failures, which, if not corrected, will preclude real and sustainable growth on the continent.

If this book was written by a 'Westerner' or a person from outside the continent, it would be easily dismissed. Label the author a 'racist', a 'colonialist', an 'imperialist' or 'white' and business as usual is easily justified. The little progress made in developing the continent has nothing to do with race or geographic location. Underdevelopment has nothing to do with the World Bank or the IMF as some grumble. There are many who hung up on historical reasons for Africa's poverty such as the slave trade or colonialisation. While all these had a hugely negative impact on the continent, nearly 60 years after independence, they are not the main factors.

The book seeks to look inwards, within the African continent, at some of our deeply entrenched ways of thinking, our behaviours, practices, values, cultures and traditions, which, if practised by any race in the world, would deliver the same result – poverty! It is not race, or the many other 'excuses' that we put forward, that makes the difference in the world in which we live.

Make no mistake, there are great things about the continent that are worth being proud of, such as our heritage, languages and diversity. There is also no doubt that the continent has made some substantial social-economic advancement over the last 50 to 60 years. However, the truth remains that Africa is still the continent that harbours most of the poor people in the world; which can't sustain its education system or healthcare; which depends on agriculture but can't adequately feed its people and has most of the internecine conflicts in the world.

With a thoughtful self-reflection, it is apparent that there is much that Africa need to change to attain meaningful development. It is time to face the reality and seek to address what is holding the continent back. The first Tanzanian president, Julius Kambarage Nyerere, once said, 'We must run, while others walk.' We cannot let anything stand in our way.

1

Vicious cycle no 1: Population growth

In the early 1980s and 1990s, what I experienced on the slopes of Mount Kilimanjaro in Tanzania where I grew up, was not all that different from the realities of many places in Africa at the time. A family of 8 to 10 children was the norm. Several families in the village had 12 to 14 children from just one couple. Every child is a blessing was the common belief, irrespective of how well or poorly the child was cared for. This thinking may still be prevalent in the rural areas and villages to this day.

Mr Audu, a Nigerian primary school teacher, who was in his mid-40s in 2016 and a father of 18 children from three wives, was interviewed by the *Financial Times*, where he expressed his pride in having 'as many children as possible'.[28] Mr Audu told the *Financial Times* further that his large family was part of his contribution to society and indicated the expectation that his children would help him in his old age. 'When I get old, I know they will take care of me,' said Mr Audu.

A 22-member family is a very large family. To sustain such a large family on a school teacher's salary is a herculean task, not to be undertaken lightly even by a high-income earner.

Similarly, parents have many children to help with farming, rearing cattle or hunting. While developed nations are thinking how best to produce more from the farms, cattle and hunting using technology, a sizable population within the continent still thinking about bearing more children in order to produce more. How would such a family – or a community or a country – compete in a world of drone-controlled drip irrigation farming? Productivity to such a family is nonexistent. To some of these families, if they owned two pieces of land located in different areas, then each piece of land – however big or small – would be a reason to take another wife and have more children, so as to cultivate the land.

No wonder then that with such 'booming' families, the United Nations estimated that the total population of the least developed countries in 2019 was projected to grow at a rate 2.5 times faster than the growth rate of the total population of the rest of the world.[29] *The Economist* recently labelled the population growth in Africa as 'dangerous'.[30] Is Africa's burgeoning population a demographic dividend or a disaster?

According to the United Nations Conference on Trade and Development report,[31] the continent was estimated to have 1.2 billion people in 2017. The same report indicated that in 1980, the continent would had an estimated population of 477 million. Literally within 37 years, the continent added around 700 million people! That is almost tripling the population in just in almost 37 years! This is a huge growth!

By 2063, the United Nations projects that the African

continent will have population of 2.92 billion, which will make up nearly 30% of the global population.[32] This is more than double Africa's population of around 1.3 billion in 2019.[33]

The year 2063 may seem far in the future. However, for countries and continents, planning for the next 20 or 30 or 50 years should be the norm. Many countries – especially developed countries – do it, such as the European Green Deal, which is a European Union climate plan and strategy aiming to be climate neutral by 2050. The action plans are concrete and followed up closely to ensure the set goals are achieved. 'I have been talking to China experts who point out that 50- to 100-plus-year plans are not unusual for many top-level Asian political leaders,' says Tim Bajarin, an American technology columnist and technology consultant, in article published on FastCompany.[34]

Many African countries have long-term plans too, however the problem has been in implementation. Perhaps the biggest difference between the plans of developed countries and African countries is whether these plans will be implemented or remain on paper. These sentiments echo what Dr Joe Abah, the former General of the Bureau of Public Service Reforms of Nigeria, said in an article published by the Africa Research Institute: 'Our problem is not planning but implementation.'[35]

The continent has never failed to have plans. A good example of a well drafted plan is the African Union's Agenda 2063, which is a commendable 50-year strategic framework for socio-economic transformation for growth and sustainable development. The failure on the other hand has many times been in implementation.

Population growth may arguably be one of the foremost causes of Africa's vicious cycle of poverty, yet it is also a key factor that, if addressed, may see the continent making headway. Let us reflect on the continent's demographics – a significant opportunity for the continent if crucial plans are made and actions are taken but a fearful liability if trade in business as usual.

Countries contributing to Africa's population growth

Between 2005 and 2018 – in just 13 years – ten African countries added almost 220 million people to the world's population – the equivalent of 15 new Zimbabwes or 14 new Senegals, or 13 new Zambias or 11 new Burkina Fasos or almost 10 Nigers – at 2018/19 population figures. If ten countries can add such 'number of new countries' within just 13 years, then the continent needs to brace for many positive and negative implications.

The table below summarises population of few countries for 2005 and 2018 from which the magnitude of the growth and projections are analysed

Table 1.1: Population growth on selected countries

Countries in Africa	Population in 2005	Population in 2018	Population increase in 13 years	Population increase in 13 years (%)
South Africa	47.9 million	57.8 million	Approx. 10 million	21%
Tanzania	38.45 million	56.3 million	Approx. 18 million	46%
Nigeria	138.9 million	195.5 million	Approx. 57 million	41%
Ethiopia	76.3 million	109.2 million	Approx. 32.9 million	43%
DR Congo	54.8 million	84.1 million	Approx. 29 million	53%
Egypt	75.5 million	98.4 million	Approx. 22.9 million	30%
Kenya	36.6 million	51.4 million	Approx. 14.8 million	40%

Countries in Africa	Population in 2005	Population in 2018	Population increase in 13 years	Population increase in 13 years (%)
Sudan	30.9 million	41.8 million	Approx. 10.9 million	35%
Uganda	27.7 million	42.7 million	Approx. 15 million	54%
Algeria	33.1 million	42.2 million	Approx. 9 million	27%
Zambia	11.8 million	17.3 milliom	Approx. 5 million	47%
Zimbabwe	12.1 million	14.4 million	Approx. 2 million	19%
Angola	19.4 million	30.8 million	Approx. 12 million	59%
Burkina Faso	13.4 million	19.7 million	Approx. 7 million	47%
Senegal	11.1 million	15.8 million	Approx. 5 million	42%
Niger	13.6 million	22.4 million	Approx. 8 million	65%
Countries in Europe				
Germany	82.4 million	82.9 million	Approx. 0.5 million	1%
France	63.1 million	66.9 million	Approx. 4 million	6%
United kingdom	60.4 million	66.4 million	Approx. 6 million	10%
Italy	57.9 million	60.4 million	Approx. 2 million	4%
Netherland	16.3 million	17.2 million	Approx. 1 million	6%

Source: World Bank

South Africa

From Table 1.1, South Africa's population increased by approximately 10 million in 13 years from 2005 to 2018. This is more than the population added by Germany, France, Italy and Netherlands combined in the same period. Each of these countries had a higher population base compared to South Africa, but added much fewer people over the same period. South Africa population has been growing by around 2.4%, which is higher than its economic growth as registered by the World Bank from 2014 through to 2020.[36] As a result of high population growth and slower growth of economy, unemployment has been increasing over a ten-year period to 2020, touching almost a third (28%) from 22% in 2008 according to the Statista.[37]

Unemployment is an intertwined problem, driven by many factors, but if the South African population continues to grow faster than the economy, then existing social-political and economic problems may take longer to abate.

Tanzania

Tanzania, is on the rise to be one of the world's populous giants, not necessarily based on current population numbers but rather population trajectory. The World Bank estimated that, in 13 years, Tanzania's population grew nearly by 18 million people – more than the entire population of the Netherlands in 2019, or Senegal or Zambia or Zimbabwe using 2019 official world bank figures.[38]

Tanzania had a lower population base in 2005 – around 38 million – compared to South Africa's base of around 48 million but added more people – 18 million compared to South Africa's 10 million people in the same period. South Africa is reproducing faster than the United Kingdom, Germany and the Netherlands combined, but Tanzania's population growth pace exceeds South Africa's.

Tanzania is very lucky that the country has been growing its economy at rate of 6 to 7% almost in the last 15 years. However, such rate of population growth is not sustainable and this trajectory may need to change for long-term meaningful progress.

To make sense of fast population growth in Tanzania, currently the country has almost similar population size to South Africa (56 million versus 57 million). However, Tanzania is projected to have more than 100 million people in 2035, and more than double its current population to 138 million in 2050 and increase its current population almost by five times to 300 million by 2100. South Africa, on the other hand, will only grow the current population to 80 million by 2100 using the same United Nations projections.[39]

NIGERIA

Nigeria, which is the largest economy on the continent, also has the largest and fastest growing population in the world. In 2005, Nigeria was estimated to have a population of 138.9 million. In 2018, its population was estimated at 195.9 million people, adding 57 million people in just 13 years. This is almost equivalent to the population of South Africa, and is greater than the population of Tanzania in 2018. In other words, Nigeria added Tanzania's or South Africa's entire population in just 13 years or added more than population of Senegal, Burkina Faso and Zimbabwe combined based on 2019 World Bank population numbers[40] in 13 years. This is certainly a large increase.

Despite being the largest economy in the continent, Nigeria also faces the challenge of high unemployment like other countries in the continent. In fact, Nigeria's unemployment dilemma is getting bigger as its population increases. PwC issued a report towards the end of 2020, which adopted official figures from Nigeria's National Bureau of Statistics showing unemployment rate of 28% with expectation of hitting 30% by end of 2020.[41] According to the same report, the unemployment rate was higher for youth aged 15 to 24, going up as high as 41%. This would be expected as Nigeria has one of the youngest populations in the world.[42]

The fact that the Nigerian economy has been growing slowly, a below 2.7% GDP growth over five year till 2020[43] is almost the rate as its population growth, which can only make socio-politico-economic progress a tougher equation to solve.

United Nations data[44] projects that Nigeria will double its current population by 2050 to 410 million people and almost quadruple it by 2100 hitting 800 million people. Brazil had almost the same population as Nigeria in 2019 and Brazil's population is projected by the United Nations to remain almost the same by 2100 when Nigeria will be adding 600 million people over the same period. This is a mouth-muting growth. Assuming Brazil's economy grows at the same pace like Nigeria, Brazilians will be by far wealthier over the same period while Nigeria will be by far less wealthy as the economic growth will be shared among the bigger population.

Ethiopia

In the same period of 13 years, Ethiopia grew its population by 32.9 million people, from 76.3 million in 2005 to 109.2 million people in 2018, as summarised in Table 1.1. The addition alone is equivalent to the entire population of Angola, which was around 31 million in 2018, or Mozambique, which had 29.5 million people in 2018, or Zambia and Zimbabwe combined with populations of 17.3 million and 14.4 million. One country multiplying itself by a factor of another country's entire population or several countries combined in just 13 years!

Despite good economic growth Ethiopia has enjoyed over time, such high population growth is likely to prove to be a strong stumbling block for its socio-politico-economic progress.

DEMOCRATIC REPUBLIC OF THE CONGO (DRC)

The Democratic Republic of the Congo is another country that added a significant number of people to the world during the same 13 years from 2005 to 2018. The figure of 29.2 million people increased in the period is 53% growth from the 2005 population. A country generating more than half of its population in 13 years is mind-boggling.

Democratic countries in Africa set the length of term a president may serve. Of Africa's 54 states, 37 democracies set terms of five years.[45] Thirteen years, then, is just over two presidential terms. Imagine increasing your country's population by 50% in the timeframe of a two-term president!

The same increase is witnessed in Uganda, which added more than the entire Zimbabwe population (15 million) in 13 years. Uganda increased its population by more than 50% over the period.

OTHER COUNTRIES

Other countries with substantial population growth between 2005 and 2018 include:

- Egypt, which added 22.9 million people from 75.5 million to 98.4 million, which is a size of Niger or more than the size of Burkina Faso or Zambia then
- Kenya, added 14.8 million people, which is equivalent to the entire Zimbabwe population at the time
- Sudan added 10.9 million people, from 30.9 million to 41.8 million
- Algeria added 9 million people from 33.1 to 42.2 million, which is twice as much the entire size of Mauritania (4.4 million in 2018) or twice as much as the entire population of Central African Republic (4.7 million in 2018).

It was not only in these few countries that this trend was observed. All countries on the continent have displayed significant population growths. Smaller countries in size and population have had their fair share of population growth. The Gambia increased by 53% from 1.5 million people in 2005 to 2.3 million people in 2018. Likewise, a country like Burundi added 3.8 million people over the period, from 7.4 million people in 2005 to 11.2 million people in 2018. The increase was more than half of its population in 2005. Similarly, Rwanda added 3.4 million to its 8.8 million people in 2005 to total a population of 12.3 million people in 2018. Togo, too, increased from 5.6 million people in 2005 to 7.9 million people in 13 years.

Future population growth

Though the population numbers discussed so far are mostly historical, the topic is even more relevant when looking at the projected demographic trends for Africa going forward.

Table 1.2: World Population Evolution by 2100

Continent	**Population (in millions)**			**Evolution 2019–2050**	**Evolution 2050–2100**
	2019	**2050**	**2100**		
Asia	4, 601.37	5,290.26	4,719.42	15%	-11%
Africa	1,308.06	2,489.28	4,280.13	90%	72%
Latin America and the Carribean	691.45	767.43	679.99	11%	-11%
Europe	747.64	710.49	629.56	-5%	-11%
North America	366.60	425.20	490.89	16%	15%
Oceania	42.13	57.38	74.92	36%	31%
World	7,713.47	9,735.03	10,874.90	26%	12%

Source: Atlas Magazine[46] and United Nations

Looking at these population projections in Table 1.2, one can safely conclude that the world population growth will be driven by Africa. All other continents or sub regions' population will almost stay the same till 2100, with a slight bump in 2050. However, Africa is going to increase its population by 90% from 2019 to 2050 and more than doubling its 2019 populous by 2100.

Sub-Saharan Africa

While the whole African continent has to check its population, the centre of the challenge lies in the Sub-Saharan Africa region. According to the UN's *World Population Prospects 2019*, the world population growth rate/pace is decreasing, even in some developing countries. However, 18 of the 46 Sub-Saharan countries are projected to double their population by 2050. The world's population is expected to increase by 2 billion people from 2019 to 2050. More than half of this global population increase is expected from Sub-Saharan Africa. This is scary. The region had an estimated population of 1 billion people in 2019. However, by 2050, the region's population is projected to double to 2.1 billion people and to nearly quadruple to 3.8 billion people by 2100.[47]

While the populations of developed countries are decreasing, with very few increasing, mainly due to migration, the populations of the poorest countries are on a doubling – and troubling – trajectory. Africa is not only going in the opposite direction compared to most developed countries, it is going there very fast. According to the UN, the populations of the least developed countries (LDCs) were growing by around 2.5% per annum in 2019 and were projected to decrease to below 1% by 2100, while major populated region of the world will experience static or negative growth of their population over the same period. In 2019, the total population of the LDCs was projected to be growing at a rate 2.5 times faster than the growth rate of the total population of the rest of the world.

According to the UN Department of Economic and Social Affairs Population Division, 'Between 2019 and 2050, the populations of 18 LDCs, all in Sub-Saharan Africa, have a high probability of at least doubling in size, while in one country, Niger, the population is projected to nearly triple by 2050. Most of the LDCs that are expected to double in population size are the world's poorest countries, with gross national income (GNI) per capita below US$1,000.'[48]

African countries that will contribute the largest absolute growth numbers in terms of population by 2100 are Nigeria, the Democratic Republic of the Congo, Ethiopia and Tanzania. Nigeria is projected to quadruple to almost 800 million people in 2100 from its current population of 200 million. Likewise, the Democratic Republic of the Congo is projected to quadruple its population to approximately 370 million by 2100.

Population and productivity

Such population projections read like dystopic, statistical fiction. Some might be tempted to think that they will not come to pass or that things will change before then. Others might cling to the myth that a large population is good for security and the economy, so population growth should not be curtailed for these strategic reasons. In the 21st century, with the advancement of technology, these myths no longer hold water. A small army such as Israel's, with its military technological capabilities, can obliterate a large army. Likewise, there are many countries with relatively smaller populations but with advanced economies and development.

A large population would make sense if it were equally productive. This is not the case with Africa. On the contrary, a significant part of the African population is young and dependent. Almost 60% of Africa's 1.3 billion population in 2019 is under the age of 25,[49] while 41% of the same base is under 15 years of age.[50] Working people between the ages of 25 and 60 make up only 35% of the continent's inhabitants. Factoring in unemployment, which is very high on the continent, the dependent population is very high. To generalise, a small part of the continent's population is working to produce wealth and, at the same time, cater for a large dependent population. This is the perfect recipe for a vicious cycle of poverty. It is nearly impossible for such a small portion of the society to produce wealth for themselves, their dependants, and at the same time, save money to invest. If anything, savings would be skimpy and ultimately investment would be meagre as well. As this cycle repeats itself over time, the continent remains in perpetual poverty.

Underscoring the severity of dependence on the continent, African Economic Outlook report for 2016[51] indicates that nine out of 10 working youth in Sub-Saharan Africa from the ages of 15 to 24, including those in urban areas, are either poor or likely to be poor. These are working young people without considering those that are not employed but they will likely be poor according to the report. This is breath-taking situation and reality.

While this is a threatening reality, population in the continent continues to increase significantly, worsening the situation. Governments' abilities to create programmes to address these challenges are limited. The two factors-high population growth and limited government resources, can only pave way for and entrench poverty in the continent. It is a vicious cycle.

Education

Are we doing enough to prepare the 41% of the population that is below 15 years of age to face the most competitive world at hand? As a continent, we are doing very badly when it comes to education. The United Nations Educational, Scientific and Cultural Organisation (UNESCO) confirms that, of all the regions in the world, Sub-Saharan Africa has the highest education exclusion.[52]

One-fifth of children between the ages of 6 and 11 are out of school, followed by one-third of youth between the ages of 12 and 14. Some 20% of children are not going to school and 33% of teenagers have not completed school. We haven't factored in the quality of education for those enrolled and going to school. This will be discussed in details in the coming chapters but the quality of education, the facilities and the ratio of teachers to students for those enrolled in schools is also sub-par. While the situation is particularly grievous in the Sub-Saharan countries, the rest of Africa is not immune.

This is not what some people in the continent would like to hear. In Africa, it may be questionable to put such facts on the table. Why display our 'nakedness'? However, our salvation lies in accepting these facts and formulating plans to address them. Unless both public and private sector stakeholders are bold enough to assess the situation and get involved in every possible way to address these challenges, the next generation might be an even bigger liability.

What the continent does today to the 41% of the population that is below 15 years will strongly determine the strength of its economies in the next decades. I would liken this 41% to a virgin land. No farmer would expect a bountiful harvest if the land had not been prepared for planting. In many parts of Africa, these children are left to fend for themselves, or left to be educated and guided by nature. 'It will all come together in the end' is the consensus silent thinking.

In Europe, children below 15 years of age make up around

15% of their population, according to the World Bank.[53] In most developed countries, in 2018, the under-15 population was below 20% of the African population of the same age. Developed countries set aside significant parts of their already substantial budgets to fund education, healthcare and programmes that support children's wellness and development. That is not the case in Africa. Funding for education, healthcare and programmes that would support children development is small and many of the programmes are left to be funded by well-wishers and donors!

In a globalised world, children from the developed and the developing world are supposed to compete equally for the same opportunities. Yet, their wellbeing, the quality of their education, healthcare resources are very different, directly affecting their potential contribution to their economy when they reach a working age.

The continent does not have enough resources to tackle the problem. Africa's economies are not growing fast enough to close the gap. At the same time, the population is growing and so is the dependence.

Population growth and poverty

With such average and meagre economic growth in the continent,[54] sharing the same small progress among the fast-increasing population can only guarantee continued poverty and further entrench the vicious cycle. Mind you, most of the economies in the world are growing and will be sharing the growth among almost the same number of people over the long term, which will keep the rest of the world population wealthier and improved. On the other hand, Africa's insufficient progress will be shared among a fast-growing population. No wonder the World Bank forecasts that, by 2030, global poverty will be largely African[55] and that Africa will be the definition of poverty.

Bill Gates once said '...more babies are being born in the places where it's hardest to lead a healthy and productive life'.[56]

There is a direct relationship between poverty and high population growth. The two phenomena are 'partners in crime'. Poverty causes high population growth and high population growth escalates poverty. Poor families cannot provide adequately for their children's education or living conditions. High death rates and higher birth rates, coupled with inadequate food provision, leading to malnutrition, which leads to stunted children – and so the cycle goes on.

While the percentage of extremely poor people has been falling in Africa, the absolute number of people in extreme poverty has been increasing. According to a report published by the World Bank in 2016,[57] poverty reduction was slowest in Africa between 1990 and 2012, much slower in poorer countries and rural areas remained poorer than cities. 'The main messages which emerge from this effort to assess poverty in Africa are both encouraging and sobering,' said Kathleen Beegle, the World Bank programme leader and co-author of the report.

When we were growing up, we could not understand how the former US President Bill Clinton and his wife Hillary could have only one child. To us, more wealth meant the ability to have more children. In many communities, when a man has made a profit on a transaction – selling some produce for a good price, for example, even if the income is temporary and seasonal – he would think about taking a new wife. Unfortunately, in the continent, the less fortunate the families the more the children and the bigger the families and vice versa is true. This reality compliments Bill Gates assertion that 'more babies are being born in the places where it is hardest to lead a healthy and productive life'.

It is mind-boggling that when a continent cannot adequately

provide for its people, it reproduces 'by far the best' compared to rest of the continents. The more it reproduces, the more it fails to cater for growing people. The more the continent, countries, families fail to provide for its people, the poorer they become! This creates intergenerational poverty. Poor parents are likely to produce poor children. No wonder some people think of this situation as a curse! It is not! It is a vicious cycle we have locked ourselves in that needs to be broken. The same cycle works for wealthy families especially in developed countries, but it works to create intergenerational prosperity.

It is two worlds apart! The fortune created by wealthy families is passed on to the children and children increase it and pass it to their children and grandchildren. Wealthy families give their best to their children. They raise them with the finest education, which builds them with an enormous capacity to produce and do well in their lives. This would have been enough; however, on top of raising them up the best way, they leave them wealth and inheritance as a strong foundation to build on. This is done consciously from the beginning. In this case, they build up intergenerational prosperity.

To the contrary, a majority in the continent give birth to as many children as possible, which results in equipping the children poorly from all fronts including education. To top it all off, these ill-prepared kids are required and expected to take care of their parents when they grow up. No doubt, there is nothing more noble and satisfying than taking care of the parents. However, it is interesting to see the perspectives of these two sets of parents. One prepares their kids the best way for the future and still leaves them fortune and inheritance while the other set prepares them poorly but still expects a lot from them in the end.

Even some wealthy families in the continent find it difficult to pass their wealth to the children and the next generation. It is very likely to be squandered and mismanaged. One is poor in Africa and passes the poverty to the next generation, but also one is well off in Africa and not almost able to pass the wealth to the future generation! This is not a curse either! This informs us of the fundamentals that need to change to break this well-entrenched vicious cycle. Let's keep the topic of generational wealth transition pending for more discussion in the coming chapters.

The more people the better?

There are those who believe that the more people, the more working hands, the more problems resolved, the more secure the country. This is a fallacy. Some proponents single out China as an example of a nation whose development was fast-tracked because of its large population. On the contrary, China had to halt its population growth in order to manage its development. Although China began promoting birth control and family planning in 1949 when the People's Republic was established, the 'official' one-child policy was formalised in 1980 and existed for 35 years until October 2015 when its end was formally announced.

It has been widely reported that the one-child policy prevented up to 400 million births.[58] This is almost equivalent to the entire European Union population as of 2019.[59] When the one-child policy was introduced, China had approximately 980 million people. China's population in 2020 was estimated to be around 1.4 billion. This means that if it were not for the one-child policy, China's population would be approaching the 2 billion mark in 2020.

Over more or less the same period of around 30 years, Sub-Saharan countries alone are projected to increase by 1.05 billion people by 2050, according to the United Nations.[60]

A projection of a doubling of the population in 30 years in many Sub-Saharan countries is plausible. We have done it before. The Ugandan population in 1990 was around 17 million. Thirty years later, in 2020, the population nearly tripled to around 45 million people. Likewise, Nigeria had a population of 95 million in 1990, and an estimated population of 200 million in 2020. The doubling trend is the same for many Sub-Saharan African countries.

Population would be considered one of the main causes of continuous poverty in the continent. Africa reproduce by far 'better' than any other continent! Economies grow and decline, countries and kingdoms rise and fall. However, population in Africa seems to know not any other direction, only growth and is projected to remain in the same course touching 2100! Growth!!

How are these countries planning to cope with this growth rate, a perfect recipe for continuous poverty and potentially severe social, political, economic and environmental liability? As a continent, we need to ensure that the populace is provided for, and that it becomes a productive force contributing to the continent's growth and not a liability. Investment in education, both in quantity and quality, has to be robust and significantly enhanced if the continent has to realise significant progress on managing population and consequently alleviating poverty. Whereas education to both boys and girls is critical, a special focus on girls has proved to bear fruits in arresting high population growth and alleviating poverty.[61] It should be education, education and education!

According to the National Academies of Science, Engineering and Medicine, 'Educating girls is a universally accepted strategy for improving lives and advancing development. Girls' schooling is associated with many demographic outcomes, including later age – marriage or union formation, lower fertility, and better child health'.[62]

Population is such a sensitive topic in the continent and in many of its communities. Population control discussion in the continent is sometimes perceived as tricks of the 'West' to depopulate the continent in order colonise it again.[63] Well-balanced, effective and ethically sound policies and programmes to address such fears and myths have to be crafted in order to make meaningful progress.

Some would say, people have survived in the past and we will survive as well. The plans should not be to survive, rather to triumph from the current levels of poverty and worsening in some parts of the continent. The continent has an enormous task ahead. We cannot wait for things to happen by chance. The future will not get easier with the current rate of population growth. It will be complex and without doing our homework, the sun may set on the continent. Preparation for the next generation is critical to reduce poverty in Africa.

By no means is this book suggesting a one-child policy for Africa, a continent of 54 countries, with diverse populations and cultures. It would take a completely different people and mindset to implement such a policy. What is the solution then? I believe, investment in education would, over time, resolve the quandary. More investment to engage the community, local societal leaders, social groups and using faith based platforms to campaign for good and safe family planning should be adopted and encouraged. Ramping up campaigns for girls' education and women's empowerment could also help in addressing population growth problem.

Figure 1.1: Vicious cycle of poverty from population growth

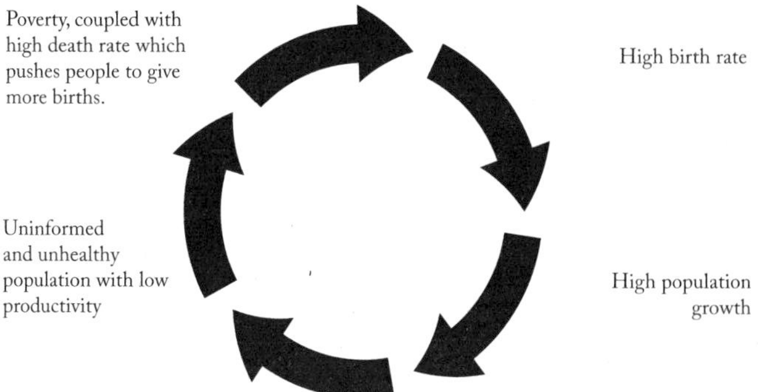
Poverty, coupled with high death rate which pushes people to give more births.
High birth rate
High population growth
Failure to provide for necessities such as education, health, etc.
Uninformed and unhealthy population with low productivity

Source: Author's own

2

Vicious cycle no 2: Poor education systems

In August 2015, my family and I had the opportunity to visit the Kennedy Space Center in the United States of America, where National Aeronautics and Space Administration (NASA) launches shuttles to space. NASA is an independent agency of the US government involved in aeronautics and space research since its inception in 1958.

I had been lucky to visit the Houston Space Center in Texas before, which is used mostly for science and educational programmes but also for fun on different spaces missions conducted by NASA. This time, accompanied by family, going to the Kennedy Space Center where NASA actually launches rockets was a thrilling experience. I was excitedly waiting to explore the centre, but my excitement to see our kids learn and how they would react was even greater.

The centre attracts more than 1.5 million visitors annually, which is very big number and equivalent to all tourists who visit Uganda annually[64] and hence expectations and excitements were high.

On board the hotel bus with other visitors who were heading to the centre, enthusiasm kicked in as we approached and saw from afar a rectangular building with the US flag on the left side and words 'NASA' on the right side of the building. We could hear other visitors talking in low voices full of excitement with some pointing at the building. It was electrifying as we approached the parking lot and we could not wait to disembark from the bus to start the tour!

As we went in, we were welcomed with large display of rocket models set up at the 'rocket garden' as they call it. The place was full of people. 'This is amazing, dad' exclaimed Praise, our eldest child. Full of excitement and anticipation, we started our tour inside the vast buildings and exhibitions. Looking at the sizes of spacecrafts, and the way the whole historic and brave missions to the space were uncovered and displayed, I could only appreciate the power of God's creation and what human beings can achieve.

From doing simulations of how things work in space shuttles to witnessing the actual shuttles that went to space, like the Atlantis, which undertook the 1985 mission and Apollo Saturn V Rocket, which is the largest rocket ever flown that took the humans to the moon.

We were also lucky enough to meet one of the astronauts who flew in the first Atlantis shuttle mission in 1985. Visibly full of wisdom, intelligence and experience, the humble astronaut explained to our children and us on how he had flown 34 types of aircrafts. No doubt, the place was a home for the bravest and finest. Alongside the physical and digital information presented, courage, determination and risk-taking imbued the atmosphere.

'The future does not belong to the fainthearted, it belongs to the brave' – President Ronald Reagan's remark was stuck on one of the walls as we walked through.

As we walked around in excitement and wonder, we were never short of reflections. How did these people achieve such feats? Certainly not only because of their bravery or willpower. One thing was clear: their accomplishments were founded on first-rate education and training. There is no nation that can release the imagination and potential of its people beyond what its education system can produce. When we see ingenuity, boundless imagination and innovations streaming from nations, then look at their education systems. There is no way the former can blossom without a commensurate investment in the size and quality of the latter.

There is a direct relationship between the economy of a country – what a country can process, produce and manage – and the quality of its education system, which is the bedrock of development. Education increases people's productivity and unleashes their creativity. It promotes entrepreneurship and technological advancement. It is central to economic emancipation and social progress. Education cuts across fields of knowledge and understanding. There is no progress without education. Indeed, the better the education, the greater the progress.

The African continent has been making some progress. The second Millennium Development Goal (MDG2) aiming at achieving universal education for primary school helped to significantly improve access to primary education in Africa and globally. According to the MDG monitor site,[65] the number of out-of-school children reduced by 50% globally between 2000 and 2015. Also, primary school enrolment improved globally from 83% to 91% in 2015 and, certainly, the fourth Sustainable Development Goal (SDG 4),[66] which also aims at improving education and lifelong learning will contribute to improving the education situation in the continent.

However, despite the good progress made, there is still much deeply entrenched poverty. Whereas educational enrolment increased, thanks to the MDGs and ongoing SDGs, the number of people living in poverty increased from 278 million people in 1990 to 413 million people by end of MDG in 2015.[67] 'Where there is abject poverty, there is minimal education. The extent of economic progress in different African countries is directly related to the progress made in education. This is why lack of education is one of the biggest and critical drivers of the vicious cycle of poverty.

Before we start citing the well-worn excuses of the slave trade, colonialism and historical oppression as reasons for our underdevelopment, let us be open-minded and reflect upon our education systems as a continent.

School enrolment and exclusion

Close to half of the current population in Africa is under the age of 18 years.[68] Yet, a large number of these children are being left behind in education. It was noted in a previous chapter that Sub-Saharan Africa has the highest rates of education exclusion in the world. According to the United Nations Educational, Scientific and Cultural Organisation (UNESCO),[69] approximately 20% of children between the ages of 6 and 11 were not in school in 2016, while 33% of young people between the ages of 12 and 14 were out of school. UNESCO estimated that 60% of youth between the ages of 15 and 17 were not going to school in Sub-Saharan Africa at the time. While we push for sustainable development on the continent, in Sub-Saharan Africa alone 20%, 33% and 60% of half of Africa's entire population has not been in school. The long-term maths of this situation is scary!

The United Nations Children's Fund (UNICEF) website accessed in March 2021, estimates that around 10.5 million Nigerian children aged 5–14 were not in school, even when primary school education was free and compulsory. This is more than the entire estimated population of Togo or Sierra Leone in 2020. It is equivalent to the entire estimated population of Namibia, Mauritania and Liberia combined. In 2017, Nigeria's Permanent Secretary of the Ministry of Education, Adamu Hussaini, echoed this figure, saying that it was 'sad to note' that 'Nigeria has the highest number of out-of-school children'.[70] At the time, every one child that was out of school out of five in the world, was from Nigeria.[71] However, never think for once that this is Nigeria's specific problem. It is only because of their high population. The problem is rampant almost all across the continent.

The loss of these millions of potential contributors to the largest economy in Africa, and in this case for the continent, is but a scratch on the surface. Primary school is where children learn the basics of numeracy and literacy. With 60% of youth aged between 15 and 17 not attending high school, the question is how the continent is going to compete in this era of artificial intelligence and fourth industrial revolution?

The US-based research institution, Brookings Institute, estimated that only 28% of secondary school youth are enrolled in schools in Africa.[72] To provide context, a child entering school in one of the 37 member countries of the Organisation for Economic Cooperation and Development (OECD) has an 80% chance of receiving some form of tertiary education, whereas for Africa, and specifically Sub-Saharan African, only 6% have a chance of receiving some form of tertiary education. Africa cannot talk about competition on the world stage or tap the many opportunities on the continent, if cannot capitalise on its own people's endowments.

With education inaccessible for such a large part of the population, and lacking the requisite skills for farming or other employment, productivity is likely to be low, with poverty the probable end result. A lack of education often results in youthful marriages. Giving birth at a young age means many such uneducated parents are ill-equipped to adequately care for and educate their children.

The more this cycle repeats, the more the rolling wheel of poverty turns, and the tougher it gets to break the cycle. It is a vicious cycle!

It is a smaller issue when this problem is taken as an individual's problem (micro level). However, collectively as a society in Africa, it is a bigger and more complex problem. Unfortunately, when it happens at such a large scale, it feels as if it is an acceptable thing to live with. After all, that 'there are so many of us' may end up been comforting thoughts and narrative. Poverty becomes part and parcel of the society if serious measures are not taken, and the vicious cycle of poverty continues. It is difficult for the continent to escape this spiral when some parents still think buying alcohol is a priority than paying for their children's school fees.

To determine the prosperity of a nation, look at its education system. There is always a direct correlation between the education system of a country and its development. No nation can develop beyond the limits of its education system. A low number of tertiary students would naturally translate into an insufficiently skilled work force and directly impact a nation's productivity.

Dropping out of school

Another major concern across the continent is the number of pupils leaving school without obtaining a minimum certification. Africa has the highest school dropout ratio in the world. Global Education Digest published by the UNESCO Institute for Statistcs, estimated that 42% of the continent's children would leave school before their last grade.[73] Around 17% were estimated to drop out of school before Grade 2. Seventeen out of a hundred pupils drop out in Grade 1. This is a sad reality. UNESCO estimated that a country like Chad had a 72% dropout ratio, while Botswana's stands at 7% and Mauritius at 2%.[74]

In South Africa's Western Cape, around 92,000 pupils were enrolled in Grade 1 in 2007. However, only 53,000 students made it to Grade 12 (Matric) in 2019.[75] Heated debates on the causes for the 39,000 missing children attributed the slump to students transferring to other regions while a significant number was attributed to dropouts. These are worrisome numbers.

The same trend is observed in many countries across Africa. In Malawi, a report by UNESCO indicated that on average there were 130 students per class in Grade 1, while there were only 64 students in the last grade.[76] This is more than a 50% drop out of students.

The situation is no different in the higher learning sector. Despite the recent boom in tertiary enrolment, the continent still lags far behind compared to regions like South Asia and Latin America. UNESCO Institute for Statistics (2020) indicated that only around 9.4% of the children in Sub-Saharan Africa were enrolled for a tertiary education in 2018,[77] while South Asia had four times higher tertiary enrolment of 25% and Latin America and the Caribbean around 51%. Quartz Africa projected in 2017 that only 6% of the children in Sub-Saharan

Africa will enrol for tertiary education, versus an 80% chance for a child in an OECD country.[78]

This is really concerning. It is impossible for the continent's nations to achieve sustainable progress with such a low percentage of their youth accessing college and universities. A particular child born in one corner of the earth has only 6% chance of getting to university while another child on the opposite side of the earth has 80% chance of enrolling to university. The two children, with these two worlds-apart opportunities, have to compete in the same world of producing goods and services, leave alone spearheading innovations and contributing in changing the world.

According to the World Bank, a global average of tertiary education enrolment was at around 39% as of 2019 while that of Sub-Saharan Africa stood at around 9%. This is more than 4 times below the world average. A continent that needs to get out of poverty as quickly as possible needs more skilled people, but not as many as needed are getting access to the required skills. Africa contributes roughly 17% of the world population.[79] However, according to *University World News*,[80] the continent only contributes around 6% of global tertiary education enrolments. This means that Africa is reproducing almost three times faster than it is educating, while the rest of the world is enrolling in higher education faster than their population growth.

We can comfort ourselves with our usual excuse of Trans-Atlantic slave trade, colonialism and neo colonialism, as there a few countries within the continent doing well in the segment of education. There is a great deal of variance in tertiary enrolment across Africa.

According to the World Bank, below are some of the few countries with enrolment of above 20% for higher learning education in Africa.[81] These include:

- Libya: 60%
- Algeria: 51%
- Morocco 39%
- Egypt: 35%
- Tunisia 32%
- Botswana 25%
- South Africa: 24%
- Namibia 23%

Only two countries in the entire continent – Libya and Algeria – are above the world average in tertiary education enrolment. There are several countries in the continent that have less than a 5% tertiary education enrolment. Even for those that have tertiary enrolment above 20% but still below world average have a long way to go.

Below are some of the countries with tertiary enrolments below 5% according to the World Bank:[82]

- Malawi: 1%
- Sierra Leone: 2%
- Central African Republic, the Gambia, Chad: around 3%
- Niger, Uganda, Tanzania, Burundi, Zambia: around 4%

Nigeria and Zimbabwe have around a 10% enrolment rate.

Comparatively, countries such as Malaysia, which got its independence in 1957, and Singapore, which got its independence in 1965 – around the same time many African countries got independence – have significantly higher learning education enrolment percentages.[83] South Korea also got independence in 1948, which was not too far out from many African countries and have significant high tertiary education enrolments.

- Malaysia: 43%

- Singapore: 89%
- South Korea: 96%

If the time of independence was the main factor, then Ethiopia with around 8%[84] tertiary education enrolment should have had over 90% as it is claimed to not have been colonialised or regained its independence in 1941 after a brief stint and fight with Italy.

We like talking about catching up with the rest of the world but how can this happen when the continent is lagging so far behind on such an important metric as education?

This has been a quantitative discussion. Let us now turn to the quality of education for those enrolled.

Learning environment

'Quality education still remains an illusion to many of Africa's youth,' said Matthew Opoku Prempeh, the Ghanaian Minister of Education, during the Accra edition of the World Innovation Summit for Education in May 2018. He reiterated that quality and access of education should be partners, 'Quality without access will lead to inequality and exclusion; access without quality will limit the potential and would not bring the desired results.'[85]

While progress has been made on increasing school enrolments, it appears that the drive to increase access to education on the continent comes from external rather than internal forces. While improvements in African children's access to education are to be applauded, the impetus to change course and confront this challenge should come from within the continent.

The prosperity, progress and, ultimately, the fate of the continent depends on appropriately educating our children for the future. Some level of anger at the status quo is probably needed to spur us to thank the 'Good Samaritans' for having done their fair share and to take charge going forward. This is not referring to stopping the good partnerships the continent has with development partners, it is about developing a stronger drive and a deep sense to wanting change of the current circumstances, owning the problem and probably saying enough is enough!

Over time, many countries on the continent have been pushing to increase enrolment. Despite the many that are still left behind, access to education in Africa has been increasing significantly, as a result of partnerships with the international community on such programmes as the Millennium Development Goals. However, an article titled 'Too little access, not enough learning' published in 2013 in *This is Africa Special Report* unpacks 'Africa's Twin Deficit in Education' –said that one-in-three children were out of school at the time of the report and 'learning levels among children who are in school are abysmal'.[86] Many children are left behind without education. However, even for those lucky enough to access it, the learning is not much. A typical vicious cycle starts kicking in.

How can a class of 50 to 150 primary school students learn effectively when some do not even have a chair to sit on in the class? As the Ghanaian Minister of Education said, success in enrolment is not an end in itself. What comes after enrolment is paramount.

Africa has the highest student–teacher ratio in the world. Most of the developed countries have a student–teacher ratio of between 10 to 15 students per teacher, with some countries such as Norway and Cuba better off with a ratio below 10:1. That means, for every 10 students, there is one teacher. In contrast, the student–teacher ratio in developing countries averages around 40 students per teacher. This is around four times the ratio of developed countries. Many countries in Africa fare far worse than the 40-student average. When the former United States First Lady Melania Trump visited a school in Malawi in 2018, the school had a student–teacher ratio of 110:1.[87] The Associated Press which covered the story quoted the minister of education at the time indicating that the school was one of the best public schools in the country. Statista indicates that the average number of students per class in Nigeria was 51 in 2018, however, in some elementary schools, the average was reported to be as high as 101 students per class.[88]

In 2018, for example, the following countries had student–teacher ratios below the world average of 23 students per teacher:[89]

- Central African Republic – 83:1
- Rwanda – 60:1
- Malawi – 59:1
- Chad – 57:1

Conversely, there are African countries that are doing relatively much better, such as:

- Mauritius – 16:1
- Tunisia – 17:1
- Egypt – 24:1.[90]

The impact of high student–teacher ratio is significant. A review of the major research conducted in the United States on class size and partly covered by the *Washington Post* in 2018 confirms the negative impact of big class sizes.

'The evidence suggests that increasing class size will harm not only children's test scores in the short run, but also their long-run human capital formation. Money saved today by increasing class sizes will result in more substantial social and educational costs in the future.'[91]

Comparatively, developed countries have far better student–teacher ratios. Europe, according to the World Bank, has an average ratio of 13 student per one teacher.[92] In addition to their lower student–teacher ratios, developed countries have better teaching equipment and facilities and well-trained and well paid teachers, which expectedly would produce by far better outcomes.

In Africa, however, in addition to high student–teacher ratio, which, by itself, impairs effective learning, we have schools that are poorly equipped, many without even a desk or a textbook in some places, nor running water or electricity. Teachers are burdened with large classes yet are poorly paid. Low morale often leads to absenteeism or lateness.

At the present age and times, there are still parts of the continent where children attend school class under the tree,[93] without own initiative to build class but hoping for donor support.[94] To set up a school under a tree is commendable effort to get education by all means. However, how can these be our realities in the 21st century when the world is talking about artificial intelligence and drone-controlled irrigation for agriculture?

This is a reality in many of the African countries. From Nigeria and Cameroon in West Africa to Kenya, Uganda and Tanzania in East Africa, as well as Angola and Mozambique in the southern side of Atlantic Ocean and Eastern side of Indian ocean, it is not difficult to find many cases of students studying under a tree.

For many in the rural areas who are lucky to be in a four-wall classroom, some have to walk several kilometres to access education. Fauzia was a fifth-grader in one of the schools in Mombasa County in Kenya in 2017.[95] According to an article done by Global Partnership for Education, which is one of the largest global fund for education, in Fauzia's school, 70% of the students walk between 7–10 kilometres to school.

'Life is difficult because some days there is no food so we sleep hungry,' Fauzia was quoted by Global Partnership for Education (GPE). 'So a lot of children arrive late—and they haven't had any breakfast, and they don't get lunch here. They only get food at night. Can you imagine trying to teach a child who has not eaten anything all day and has walked so far?' Fauzia's teacher was quoted in the GPE article.

Whether it is Fauzia in Kenya, or Rockcilia, a girl in Zambia who used to wake up at 4.30am to walk 7 kilometres to school every day,[96] or Bashadu, a girl in Ethiopia who has to choose to skip school for two days to go to fetch water 20 kilometres away,[97] it is not something uncommon in many Sub-Saharan countries.

From a student walking several kilometres a day to school without having eaten breakfast to sitting in a classroom packed with students three to five times the world average ratio. Taught by a teacher who is very lowly paid and with large family to look after and probably lowly motivated. As if it is not enough, the school will have no electricity nor running water and there could be only one text book which the teacher uses to teach and if they are lucky to have few other books, will be for sharing in groups. Definitely the school would not have a library and such vocabulary does not even exist for many of those students as there will be no library even in the nearby small township let alone in their own community. It would be lucky if the school would have toilets and for those that have, it will be a few pit latrines shared by as many as 100 to 200 students per one hole.

A survey conducted by UNESCO Institute for Statistics on school resources and learning in Africa[98] revealed sobering results in 2016. The results indicated that one in three (33%)

of primary schools in many African countries did not have toilets. There were several countries in West and Central North Africa where more than 50% of schools did not have toilets, while some countries fared well with zero percentage of school without toilets, like in Zimbabwe, Botswana, Uganda, Tunisia and Ethiopia to name a few. There were countries in the report with more than 80% of the primary schools that did not have toilets. How sobering are these realities!

At the end of the school day, a student from such school will have to walk several kilometres back home, where a meal may or may not be forthcoming. This student will have to repeat this daily routine for close to around 200 school days of the year.

How can children in such conditions start to imagine, create, innovate and change their world?

The results of such learning environments are unsurprising. Sub-Saharan Africa has 27% of the world's illiterate adults and adult literacy rates are below 50% in 17 African countries.[99] In ICT language, they say, 'garbage in, garbage out'. We cannot reap differently from what we sowed.

The goal of education is to produce a generation of people with the skills, knowledge and values that they need to realise their potential, and thus drive socio-economic growth in their communities and countries. However, in Africa, the discussion is still on how many of the people cannot read or write. According to the World Bank, there are countries in Africa still with illiteracy rates of 60% among the adults above 15 years of age by 2019.[100] It is very difficult to make meaningful progress in a nation where more than half of its population cannot read and write. Of the 14 countries in the world by 2019 whose 50% of population could not read or write, 13 of the countries were in Africa.

The continent improved school enrolments, which is a big

step. Nevertheless, the quality of instruction after enrolment requires a fundamental overhaul if Africa is to take significant strides towards sustainable development.

The quality of education in Africa is deficient from pre-primary to tertiary institutions – colleges, universities and vocational courses.

Given the low level of admissions to the universities and colleges, one would expect a favourable ratio of students to lecturers. Unfortunately, this is not the case. Quacquarelli Symonds (QS) is one the world's leading providers of analytics and insight to the global higher education sector. QS estimates that, in Sub-Saharan Africa, there are around 50% more students per lecturers than the global average.[101] While it is generally accepted that the size of the class at lower levels of primary or secondary school education affects the quality of education, the same debate is not fully settled at the tertiary level. It could be a compounding problem. Poorly prepared students from lower levels, with limited resources, such as library books, computers, labs and basic infrastructure, insufficient teaching staff, encounter large classes at the university level. Large classes limit the number of group or individual student presentations a lecturer can accommodate. Many lecturers resort to multiple-choice-question-type assessments and exams, where students fill in the blanks or provide short-form answers as a result of the class size.

An article on the *University World News* website quoted one agricultural science professor from a West African university, who said he had removed a laboratory component from his course because of the class size. Instead, he brought the laboratory equipment to the lecture room to demonstrate how to use it. 'How could the students learn how to use a soil tester by merely looking at it? But that was my way out of the quagmire of inordinate enrolment,'[102] the professor was quoted in the article.

The continent has few graduates. We desperately need to increase university enrolments to increase the number of graduates. Unfortunately, when we increase their number, we impair the quality of education and hence we produce more graduates with less education. Imagine, an agricultural science graduate who completes his/her studies in a class where he/she has only seen how soil is tested but has never actually tested it. The same graduate is expected to help the ailing agricultural sector on the continent and, at the same time, compete with agricultural science graduate from Israel, for example, who may have studied and used technology such as drip or drone irrigation.

It is not the size of the class alone that negatively affect the quality of higher learning institutions in Africa. There are many policy and management actions that have contributed to the current, continuing state of affairs.

In 2017, Kamau Ngotho penned an article for the Kenyan daily newspaper *Nation* with the title, 'Clamour for degrees killed our education system'.[103] The article detailed how the higher learning education system had changed in Kenya over time. Much is applicable to other African countries too from the article.

> On Sunday, I watched cabinet secretaries Fred Matiang'i and Joe Mucheru explain on television what went wrong with our education and examination systems. I couldn't agree more.
>
> Talk to any corporate employer and, if they're frank enough, will tell you one of their biggest challenges today is to get qualified staff, yes, qualified, as opposed to merely having academic papers.

...

Where did the rain start beating us?

GRADUATES

The first goof we made was to create a nation that believes everybody must go to university and be a graduate.

Never mind how well baked the graduate is. The issue was to graduate, period.

So, as a nation, we embarked on mass-production of 'graduates'.

We began by converting every good middle-level college to a university.

COLLEGES

We did away with great colleges like the Kenya Polytechnic whose higher diploma in engineering had better premium in the labour market than an undergraduate degree.

We killed Jomo Kenyatta College of Agriculture and Technology, which was supposed to give us high-skilled, hands-on diploma holders to launch us into the still elusive agro-industrial economy status.

We killed the Kenya Science Teachers College, the Kenya Technical Teachers College, and any other middle-level college of repute you can remember.

All we wanted were university 'graduates' so to hell with middle-level colleges.

Next we embarked on opening up campuses of this or that university at every available space in town.

We'd open university 'campuses' atop garages and next door to the fish market.

...

At the moment we have more than 70 public and private universities, more than in some of the Asian-Tiger countries.

In South Korea, for example, university education is just for few elites.

The chaps building the cars for our roads and electronics in our houses are diploma and certificate holders.

The few college graduates they have are in labs designing the next generation of i-phone

...

This is unlike the old days when we had as many diploma and certificate extension officers out in the field helping modernise our agriculture for more productivity.

Today they're rare species but we have an army of agriculture 'degree graduates' idle in the streets.

EXAM CHEATING

The craze to mass-produce degree graduates inevitably had to give birth to exam cheating.

Because a degree certificate was all that mattered, we began to coach, not teach, our children to 'pass' examinations at all levels – KCPE, KCSE, and university.

Then we advanced to stealing the exams.

After all, why do the coaching to pass when you can buy the answer sheet on the last day before the exam?

> In short, let's go back to the basics and re-introduce competence and skills-based education as opposed to exam/papers-based 'education'
>
> That way, we won't have to mourn that we have very few 'As' and so many 'Ds'.
>
> Instead we will celebrate that we're making good use of every 'A' and every 'D' – even 'E' to move the country to next level of development'[104]

Mr Ngotho was not belittling university education or even university graduates for that matter. The scenario captured in his article is no different from the trend followed in many other countries on the continent. Each country is in a race to produce graduates. How those graduates support the continent's emancipation from poverty is another story. According to *University World News*,[105] the move to convert polytechnics to universities started in South Africa in 2004, followed by a wave of other countries such as Ghana, Kenya, Tanzania and Nigeria. Is it not a sin to convert technical/polytechnic colleges to universities. However, a pertinent question remains unanswered – are technical skills less needed in Africa or do we have too many technical or polytechnic colleges?

The African Union Agenda 2063 report on African critical technical skills confirms that in the last two decades, the development of critical technical skills in Africa was not given its due weight.[106] It reported a 'serious' shortage of critical technical skills to support the initiatives of the first ten years of the implementation of Agenda 2063.

Whereas technical, vocational and polytechnic colleges contribute significantly to developing the critical technical skills needed on the continent, the move to convert some of these colleges to traditional universities counteracted our needs. The wave of conversions seemed to flow from a sudden realisation that Africa was short of graduates, and countries needed to act fast, despite the fact that not all the existing graduates were employed. As always, with the 'justifiable' excuse of limited budget, alternative paths were limited. Converting technical colleges to universities was the quick fix to fast-track the increase in university enrolments.

Professor Goolam Mohamedbhai, who is the former Secretary-General of the Association of African Universities, once said:

> While Africa unquestionably needs an increased pool of excellent professional engineers, it equally needs an even greater number of practically trained, versatile technicians, not only to support the professional engineers, but equally to service and initiate small- and medium-scale industries, in order to create employment, improve the quality of life and make fuller use of local resources.[107]

Is the continent going against the current? While many African countries have been converting technical, vocational and polytechnic colleges to universities, China made a radical decision in 2014 to convert 600 general universities into polytechnics. The then Vice-Minister of Education in China said, 'There is an urgent need to reform our current education system, which has been struggling to provide high-quality talents with skills and knowledge that meet demand at the production frontline.'[108]

China realised that for growth to rise and unemployment to fall, more technically trained graduates were needed. According to *University World News*, vocational college graduates had a slightly higher average starting salary compared to graduates from China's top 100 universities.[109]

From 1981 to 2008, China lifted around 600 million

people out of poverty – half of Africa's population. It did this, not by giving its citizens grants, but through various policy interventions, especially in the rural areas, as well as improving skills and education standards. Western countries did not rush to invest in China only because of cheaper labour, but because of its skilled and productive workforce.

Notwithstanding the conversion of technical colleges to increase enrolment at universities, the problem of university scarcity remains in Africa, as its youthful population grows. For example, 'In Nigeria, fewer than 40% of university applicants are regularly admitted to Nigerian universities, leaving an estimated one million students without any university placement.'[110]

Now with fewer technical colleges – or none – the only option for many is to go to university or remain on the streets. As many strive to be accepted at African universities, helping us to tick the box for enrolment, the limited number of universities remains overcrowded and the question of whether students are learning effectively lingers in our minds. Believing that everybody must go to university is probably where the 'rain started beating us' in the words of Kamau Ngotho. It is a vicious cycle within a vicious cycle. We find ourselves with inadequate technical skills and 'half-baked' graduates. This is the deep end of the lake.

Looking at the number of graduates as a percentage of the population, one would conclude that Africa has a shortage of graduates.[111] Yet, many cannot find a job.[112] But, how can we say that Africa has too few graduates when many are jobless? From politicians to socio-economic analysts, all lament the shortage of jobs on the continent. The problem lies in a mismatch between skills production and the needs of the labour market. 'The recent worrisome trend in African higher education is the low percentage of graduates in areas of engineering, agriculture, health and science.'[113]

The links in this twisted chain of things form a vicious cycle. Low education levels adds into levels of illiteracy. Illiteracy leads to low primary and secondary school enrolments, which do not address the illiteracy levels quickly enough. Those who are enrolled face overcrowded classrooms, tough school environments with no enough books, running water and too few teachers.

High levels of dropouts and low passes means many do not get to cross to college or university. Of the few who do well at secondary school, many do not get the opportunity to go to technical colleges or universities because of infrastructure incapacity. Those few who make it to college or university face overcrowded lecture rooms and classes because facilities are too few for the lucky few. A number of those who graduate do not find jobs. Self-employment becomes a challenge for the majority because of the type and quality of education received from primary to tertiary level.

As a result, there are many people on the streets that barely contribute to the desperately needed growth of African economies. When these economies are not growing fast enough, they do not create enough job opportunities to cater for the large number of unemployed and cannot fund education sufficiently. Lack of enough funding to education breeds low quality of education, which leads into illiteracy and the cycle repeats itself.

Unfortunately, more spill-overs further impact these cycles. Many of those who are left behind – the majority of them without a good education – are left with few options, such as marrying at a young age and bearing several kids who are supposed to be lucky enough to make it on their own. As a result of early marriages, kids are not well taken care of, which results into a series of other health development issues.

With the high birthrates, the population increases faster than governments can accommodate. This leads the said society to spinning helplessly in the never-ending vortex of poverty. These are the realities in both urban and rural areas in the continent.

As if all this is not enough, some of those that overcome the odds and achieve academic success are snapped up by developed countries – with Africa's blessing. In many cases, it is us who encourage our best and brightest to go abroad, as though Africa cannot retain or is not worthy of their great talents. The African Union estimates that about 70,000 skilled professionals emigrate from the continent per year.[114] The situation is worse in Sub-Saharan Africa, which needs those professionals the most.

The World Economic Outlook report done by the International Monetary Fund (2016) indicated that 'brain drain was acute for Sub-Saharan Africa'.[115] In line with this, Thabo Mbeki, the former South African president once labelled Africa's brain drain 'frightening' and said Africa had lost 20,000 academicians and 10% of highly skilled information technology and finance professionals.[116]

BBC News had a debate in 2012 whether there were more Malawian doctors in Manchester in the United Kingdom than in Malawi.[117] These are sobering realities that continue to strangle the continent. Some might argue that exporting African talents is a noble cause and good for the continent as well as there are many countries around the world that have benefited and grown their influence through such moves.

Unfortunately, in Africa, the talents are not exported but rather migrate, as most do not come back. The words in the Holy Bible in Mark 4:25 have a particular resonance here: 'To those who have, more will be given. From those who have little, even that they have will be taken from them.'

Andreas Schleicher, the head of education at the

Organization for Economic Co-operation and Development (OECD) and the founder of the Programme for International Student Assessment (PISA) once said:

> ...knowledge and skills have become the global currency of 21st century economies, but there is no central bank that prints this currency. Everyone has to decide on their own how much they will print. Sure, it's great to have oil, gas and diamonds; they can buy jobs. But they'll weaken your society in the long run unless they're used to build schools and a culture of lifelong learning. The thing that will keep you moving forward is what you bring to the table yourself.[118]

The continent desperately needs a complete paradigm shift in our thinking and our actions if we are to meaningfully engineer and bolster economic growth and deliver true emancipation from poverty. We need a complete change in the way we approach our education, from the education system itself to budget allocation, resourcing and execution. Mass quality education is a must for the continent as we seek to nurture our talents and promote innovation and creativity.

There is a Chinese proverb that goes: 'If you want one year of prosperity, then grow grain, and if you want 10 years of prosperity, then grow trees, but if you want 100 years of prosperity then grow people.'

We must develop a 'productive' anger at this woeful state of affairs and say enough is enough. We cannot continue being the laughing stock of the world. Rather than preventing our talent from going abroad, we need to cultivate a conducive environment to which they can return and stay.

As a continent we must start working on our education system, now; not later.

Professor Fanuel Tagwira, the Permanent Secretary for the

Ministry of Higher and Tertiary Education of Zimbabwe once said: 'Our young people are running away from Africa while the Chinese and Europeans are running to Africa. It means we are not equipping our youths with the right skills to see what those coming to Africa are seeing.'

The continent should not be talking about having many graduates. No. We should be talking about education that will transform the inner person, and bring to light the gifts, talents and abilities within, for the greater good of the continent and humanity. We must eradicate the poverty within.

'That way, we won't have to mourn that we have very few "As" and so many "Ds". Instead we will celebrate that we're making good use of every "A" and every "D" – even "E" – to move the country to the next level of development.' – Kamau Ngotho[119]

There is no nation that can release the full potential and imaginations of its people and the nations beyond what its education can produce. When we see ingenuity, with unmatched imaginations and innovations steaming from nations, just look at its education system. The former can never blossom without a matching the size and quality of the later.

Figure 2.1: Vicious cycle of poor education systems

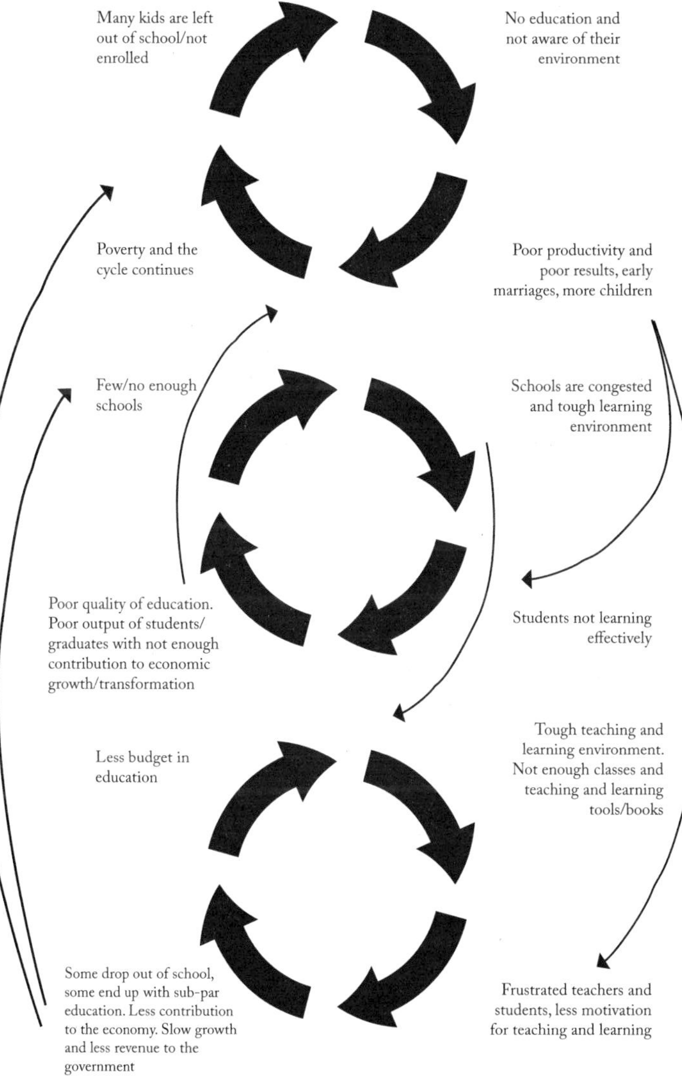
Many kids are left out of school/not enrolled
No education and not aware of their environment
Poor productivity and poor results, early marriages, more children
Poverty and the cycle continues
Few/no enough schools
Schools are congested and tough learning environment
Students not learning effectively
Poor quality of education. Poor output of students/ graduates with not enough contribution to economic growth/transformation
Less budget in education
Tough teaching and learning environment. Not enough classes and teaching and learning tools/books
Some drop out of school, some end up with sub-par education. Less contribution to the economy. Slow growth and less revenue to the government
Frustrated teachers and students, less motivation for teaching and learning

Source: Author's own

3

Vicious cycle no 3: Blaming others and dependence

Dependence

I once worked briefly for a donor-funded water project in a region on the continent, where water wells were drilled for the villages and communities. After completion, the project was plagued with sustainability concerns. The donor had funded the project but service and maintenance were not included, although the beneficiary community expected as much. Communities were supposed to take care of the well and maintain them by contributing a small token of money per month as they use the water. Unfortunately, most of the wells were left to dry or many of the pumps were not functioning.

Some of the communities did not set up an initiative to charge the smallest amount possible to help service the pump and the well. Those who did set up the groups, a significant number of members did not contribute anything. 'The people are poor,' the village leader said. People were poor, it was true, but this could have been an opportunity to set up a small vegetable farm near the well that would create revenue to maintain the well. The minds of these communities were for the pumps and wells to be serviced by the donors who funded the project.

A definition of 'dependence' by Mkwazi Mhango, a researcher and an author of several books, sums up it all. It states that 'dependence is any chronic behaviour affecting a person or society so as to force it perpetually to succumb to depending on someone or society to address his, her or its needs and sometimes problems, in order to develop.'[120]

In Africa, dependence is almost institutionalised; it is part of every community. To actually write against such a mindset, one needs a stony heart, as you are likely to be seen as callous and selfish. However, this is the mindset that has manacled us, lethally injecting a dependence culture into our bones and infusing it into our bloodstreams. Dependence is devouring the continent.

When dependence is carried for far too long, it creates what others call 'dependence syndrome'. This is a situation where aid beneficiaries lose impetus for work or do work intetionally to qualify for aid.

An article published by the University of California Press in 2015,[121] based on a food security research conducted in one of the African countries that had been mired in violent conflict, revealed a persistent 'culture of dependency' within the communities.

'The social-structural dependency of rural communities on international non-governmental organizations for basic foodstuffs; a so-called "culture of dependency" that our informants claimed had taken root in rural areas, so that local people had lost old habits of autonomy and self-reliance' reads part of the article.

Dependency syndrome is not only reflected in war or conflict-torn countries, it also part of communities in stable countries. Tanzania got into the lower middle income status in July 2020 ahead of its 2025 plan. As expected, there were celebrations on crossing this important developmental mark since the nation came into being. There were also debates at the same times on whether the average person's life had changed as significantly as crossing the mark sounded.

Again, there were debates on the negative implication of attaining the status and whether the country should celebrate. Some people contended that getting into middle income status was going to get donors reduce their support to the country and also make borrowing more expensive for the country as favours that are given to low income countries would disappear. Their argument implied that the country 'should have remained in the same status' in order to continue enjoying donor supports and aid given to the low-income countries. The same applied to Kenya and Ghana in 2014 and 2011 respectively when they moved to lower middle-income countries status. The same arguments were discussed in their countries. This is a perfect dependence syndrome.

It is indisputable that Africa has been dependent, unfortunately not on its own people but on outsiders for decades. Some would say the continent has been overly dependent on foreign aid and support. Over the last 60 years, Africa has received over US$1 trillion of foreign aid.[122] This is almost half of the current entire Africa economy – GDP. Many of the African countries' fiscal budgets are dependent on foreign aid especially for some key sectors such as health, water and education. Some countries such as Mozambique and Malawi have as high as 60% of the health expenditure supported by donors.[123] Many other Sub-Saharan African countries are still dependent on donors on their health expenditure but below 20%.[124]

The continent accounts for a disproportionate share of the global disease problems,[125] which should have called for more investment in the healthcare system, but it is the sector that many governments allocate the least amount of resources to. Annual per capita health expenditure in the continent averaged US$80 in 2016 while the Organization for Economic Co-operation and Development (OECD) countries averaged at US$4,000. This is shame on the continent.

In countries like Kenya, Tanzania and Nigeria, just to mention a few, are highly dependent on donors for the working of their healthcare system. Donors in Kenya spend between one and half times to two times government expenditure on health.[126] More than 90% of the Tanzania HIV/AIDs funding come from external sources.[127]

Healthcare systems in many African countries have been supported by donors and well wishers since independence, and there is no concrete plan and actions to reverse this situation any time soon. Nigeria is the largest economy in Africa. The country almost doubled its income per person (per capita income) in the last 15 years increasing from US$1,000 per capita in 2004 to US$2,229 in 2019.[128]

This is certainly a good progress and can pat ourselves on the back, but if we compare it to China, it is not a good enough progress. China grew its capita income from US$1,500 in 2004 to US$10,200 in 2019, which is almost seven times growth. Despite the modest economic growth, Nigeria registered over the period and at the same time becoming the largest economy in the continent in 2013/2014, the country has constantly grappled to finance its health sector. Most vaccination programmes, malaria, tuberculosis, HIV/AIDS, and maternal and child health still remain almost entirely dependent on foreign donors.[129]

'The health sector has suffered from chronic underfunding for many years now. We are even behind South Sudan, Angola, and Ethiopia,' said Isaac Adewole, Nigeria's health minister.[130]

If donors withdrew their funding, the healthcare systems of many sub-Saharan countries would stagnate and likely collapse.

It is the same trend with education system in the continent. It is also highly dependent on foreign donations and support. In 2017, 20 sub-Saharan countries were among the 26 countries worldwide that relied on donor funding for more than 20% of their health spending,[131] while in three other countries donors were contributing more than those governments in secondary education.

The situation is even worse for other sectors like water. Water and sanitation are basic essentials for human beings, yet in Sub-Saharan Africa, 42% do not have access to basic water supply and 72% are without basic sanitation facilities.[132] The Democratic Republic of the Congo is estimated to have up to 52% of Africa's surface water reserves, and accounts for an estimated 23% of Africa's internal renewable water resources.[133] However, less than 50% of its people have access to drinking water and about 20% to sanitation.[134] Donors provide nearly 99% of the water sector finance in the DRC.[135]

A senior economist at the Institute of Economic Affairs in Ghana calls this level of dependence an 'addiction'.[136] We fail to think for ourselves and wait to be supported. We have the rest of the world do our thinking, fund researches and find solutions for us.

Since large part of the continent can depend on others to think for it and to solve their problems, why should invest in their people? The continent is full of creative and talented people, but why do we not make better use of their talents? Even when some governments try to invest in building the capacity of their people, as a result of the dependence 'addiction', many participants attend training courses simply for the daily allowance, and if outside the country, for shopping, but not for learning and development.

This is the dependence that Africa must relinquish in favour of building a stronger system with institutional support. Unfortunately, many African nations do not have a plan to wean themselves from the dependence addiction. Where there are such plans, implementation is so far off that economic self-sufficiency is a will-o'-the-wisp rather than true north.

Take the Abuja Declaration as an example. In 2001 heads of states of African Union countries met in Abuja, Nigeria and made firm pledge to increase their health budgets to 15% of their annual budgets. This was meant to strengthen Africa's health systems as the sector was highly underfunded. Ten years later, in 2011, only two countries, Rwanda and South Africa, had achieved the agreed target.[137] In 2016, 15 years later, 19 African countries were spending less on health as a percentage of their public spending than in the early 2000s. Twenty years down the line in 2021, many countries in the continent are still grappling and wrestling with the similar health challenges faced in early 2000s.[138]

Seldom is health a priority in terms of budget allocation and actual fund disbursement. Health budgets in many countries in Africa are usually small but only a fraction of it is actually allocated, straining the sector even further. This is to say African dependence is not on paper dependence. It is well entrenched in people's minds and beliefs. The thinking seems to be that there will always be a basket of funds and donations that will take care of this important sector.

Dependence has denied the a chance to be 'players' in the

world economy and confined it to remaining perpetual recipients. We import most of the things from outside the continent.[139] We are net consumers of what others produce. We depend on others for most goods and even services. Dependence delivers poverty and poverty triggers dependence. Since we depend on donors to sustain our health sector and education sector, and support our water and sanitation sector just to mention a few, we do not budget enough to support these sectors. Even when we budget, we only disburse a portion of the funds because we know someone will come to rescue us. This way, the continent remains dependent on donors to fund these key sectors.

The more we depend on support, the less attention we pay to the sector in funding it. This is one of the ways the vicious cycle of poverty continues on the continent. There has never been a country in the world that was developed by depending on another country to freely fund its development. With the high levels of dependence, sustainable development is almost impossible.

An astonishing number of project papers are written in Africa each month in order to impress donors. So many people rack their brains and scratch their heads to find innovative ways to convince and attract foreign aid. If the same level of thinking and focus put on project papers were applied to come up with homegrown solutions to the continent's problems, Africa would have made significant progress in development.

If aid was a game changer in Africa, then the continent would have been different. We are living in the shade of dead aid. Zambian-born Dambisa Moyo was the head of economic research and strategy for Sub-Saharan Africa at Goldman Sachs. In her book, published in 2009, entitled *Dead Aid: Why Aid is Not Working and How There is a Better Way for Africa*, she argues that 'Despite the more than US$1 trillion in development aid given to Africa in the past 50 years ... that aid has failed to deliver sustainable economic growth and poverty reduction – and has actually made the continent worse off.'[140]

Dambisa Moyo says, 'aid has helped make the poor poorer, and grow slower.' Thus, foreign aid is deemed as cultivating the dependency syndrome, which is seen as a retrogressive element that stifles Africa's ability to stand on its own considering that Africa is richly blessed with natural resources and indigenous knowledge systems that can sustain it if properly managed. Hence, aid cannot be viewed as a remedy.

As much as Dambisa Moyo would be correct that aid has helped to make the poor poorer, blame should not be on aid. We have chosen to blame aid and donors instead of 'blaming' and working on our dependence mindsets. It is the mindset to depend on aid is to be denunciated more than the aid itself.

There is no self-sufficient nation on Earth that can exist without depending on another nation. Countries and continents are interdependent. Make no mistake, even the most powerful individuals and countries in the world may need help, at times. For example, over 60 countries and organisations supported the United States during Hurricane Katrina in 2005.[141]

Several African countries contributed to help the United States quickly recover from the crisis. Gabon, a very small country in Africa, pledged US$500,000. Djibouti, a country of less than a million people, pledged US$50,000 and Nigeria pledged US$1 million. This display of solidarity was an important gesture that underscored the mutual relationships, shared support and intertwined destinies that bind nations together as human beings on Earth. At times, an individual, society or a country may need support, no matter the financial status or background, race, religion and even history. Giving and receiving support is part of being a human. However, this is not what the book is referring to when it comes to Africa.

The same need to support each other is very much accentuated with the gesture and backing that we witnessed during the outbreak of the Covid-19 pandemic in 2019. Developed countries like Italy, Spain and the United States received different gestures of support from different countries and organisations. This is normal and happens from individuals to countries.

Sometimes we have used these environments and situations to justify dependence on aid. This is totally different.

The support given to Italy during the Covid-19 first wave would be a classic example here. As the Covid-19 pandemic unfolded, Italy was one of the first countries that was hit very hard. Hospitals were overwhelmed. There were pictures of people laying on beds along verandas and corridors. The number of deaths were exponentially increasing each day. All the world's eyes and ears turned to Italy.

There was insufficient surgical masks, gowns, let alone, ventilators to suffice the acute need that was growing hour after hour. It was a terrible situation to follow through the news. Many countries and organisations weighed in to rescue the situation; some sending surgical masks and tools, others sending doctors and nurses, while others supporting with ventilators. A large number of well wishers supported with words of prayers as the situation was almost getting out of hand. All the supports significantly helped to stabilise the situation though deaths continued in the country, but at least the rate of infections and death were coming down.

Now, the above situation is not a dependent circumstance. Although the country was in a dire state and was almost evident that things could have fallen apart without the support, but was a timely support that anyone from individual, organisations, society or country could need. Their health system would not need continuous support to function properly.

In some instances, dependence on foreign aid in key sectors has reduced over time across Sub-Saharan Africa.[142] However, poverty has not reduced much.[143] It is only when we determine to break the shackles of dependence and act on that determination can our progress be truly celebrated.

Dr Jong-Dae Park, South Korean Ambassador to South Africa and former ambassador to Uganda had this to say on support amassed for Africa: 'Even scholars and practitioners involved in the development of Africa seem to be still baffled by the "African paradox" after many decades since the world began trying to address Africa's plight. In the history of humankind, no continent has drawn such worldwide, collective attention and support on a sustained basis as Sub-Saharan Africa.'[144]

African dependence is not only on paper, it is a mindset deeply rooted from within that even when we are capable of doing something on our own, we will still find a way to hitch a free ride.

So far, the book has been focusing on dependence at a national level. However, the mentality of dependence begins at an individual and community level, and expands to the national level. This is a difficult space to navigate. There is a Swahili saying which translates thus: 'A dependent relative will die poor.' This sounds rather callous and seems to discourage supporting those in need. On the contrary, the idiom does not have anything to do with helping or not helping one another. It does, however, point to the reality that those addicted to a dependent mindset will never succeed.

If the person being supported believes he or she cannot succeed without being supported and thus does nothing to change their circumstances, then the 'addiction' to dependence flourishes and vicious cycle of poverty rolls on. The same principles apply to countries dependent on foreign aid and investment. It is little wonder then that after 50 or 60 years of independence, many African countries are still poor. There is almost nothing wrong with the aid or the aid giver, but there is something wrong with the aid recipient.

In most cases, when a child is born in Africa, he is sure to receive an inheritance from his parents – whether a piece of land, a herd of cattle, sheep or goats, a house, a car or simply clothes. This is a tradition practised in many African countries. Many young men set themselves up with whatever they get from their parents. There are also many who simply wait for their inheritance as they have no plans of their own for their future.

Particularly in the rural areas of Africa, most families have land. In many African communities, people aspire to own a plot of land and, later on, a house. For those living in the villages, many young people wait to be apportioned a piece of land by their parents, who inherited the land from their parents. The same piece of land is divided amongst the children and the grandchildren until it can no longer be divided.

What heirs do with these farms or pieces of land is an important question. Unfortunately, they do the same that their grandfathers did. They cultivate the soil for subsistence living. The plots of land diminish in size as they are divided among the heirs, and thus the land may not be large enough to sustain the extended family, which, instead of prospering, ultimately becomes worse off.

Children depend on getting a piece of land from their parents to farm. Parents depend on the support of their children when they grow old. This approach amounts to sharing the same poverty over time and so the cycle of poverty continues.

In various communities in the developed countries, parents

loan their graduate child a car or teach them to acquire their first assets on their own. Some parents go even further and lend their children the university tuition fees, and their children faithfully work hard to pay back the loan. This builds strong independent minds.

A Canadian friend visited Tanzania when I was in my final year at the university. He had just finished his studies in Canada and was visiting Tanzania for a few weeks. He told me how he was working hard to repay a car loan from his father. He would even budget less for food to pay back his father's loan. I was pleasantly surprised. How could a parent lend money to his son, who had just graduated, instead of giving him the car for free? This would not happen in many parts of the continent. If a family is wealthy in Africa, the children are gifted with the latest model cars their parents can afford. These are two different value systems. The Canadian friend would seek to work harder to pay his father's loan but also to establish his own life, largely creating an independent mindset. Comparatively, an African child from a wealthy family would relax and wait to inherit from his parents, hence cultivating a dependence mindset. Two different mindsets. Same applies to family, community and a country. It firms up the Swahili saying *'mtegemea cha nduguye hufa masikini'*, which literaly means 'A dependent relative (community/country) will die poor'.

As noted from the previous chapter, a significant number of parents send their children to school so that they will help them when they are old. Such parents are already creating dependent minds when they send their children to school. It is likely they will not invest or save for the future because they are expecting their children to take care of them. This is normally justified as future sacrificed saving for education because of low incomes and subsistence living of many in the continent. This does not mean that children should not support their parents or vice versa, there is nothing nobler than doing it exceedingly. However both older and younger generations should not be held back by a mindset of dependency.

Developed countries raise their children to not be reliant on their own parents – a master class on independence. Not only do such values create independent people but also people who will seek to increase the wealth in their own families instead of just sharing in what their parents have. Moreover, if children are independent in most material aspects, their parents are free to continue growing their own wealth, and thus, as parents age they will be less dependent on their children.

As if dependence was not enough to hold the continent back, we also engage in the blame game. We are full of excuses. If one listens to developmental conversations in the continent, it sounds as if Africans share no responsibility for the hardship and penury so many of us experience. Blame is directed at 'the West': colonialism, imperialism, apartheid, the International Monetary Fund (IMF) and the World Bank. Most of our failures are caused by colonialism and colonialists. These are the stories we sing and pour, like cement, into our children. Many of our children grow up being told of our inability to do things because of the West or others who hold us back. We are what happened to us and not what we choose to become. And so we instill a sense of hate, of self-defeat, of victimhood, rather than a sense that we are masters of our own fate with the future in our hands.

There has been much discussion about decolonising the minds of Africans. We talk more about colonialists and imperialists oppressing us and stealing from us, than we talk about our own systems and ways of living that have gotten us where we are. The more we blame colonialism and history for our current circumstances, the more we fail to accept responsibility and take action. The more we talk about colonialism in our schools and in our public and daily discourse, the more it becomes part and parcel of our daily lives. While the slave trade, colonialism and apartheid were responsible for the great human tragedy, and while Africa is still unfairly treated in some ways by the West, dwelling on such grievances limits our ability to look forward to the future. While such systems, organisations and powers are not guiltless, they are in no way largely responsible for our current poverty.

On 4 July 2018, French President Emmanuel Macron might have regretted tweeting: '60% of the Nigerian population is aged under 25. That's 60% of the population, which, like me, did not witness colonisation. We are the new generation. We are going to dispel prejudice by rebuilding a new future through culture.'

The tweet generated a huge backlash from many Nigerians and other Africans. Some poured their anger on Macron and the Western nations. Many of the responses reminded me how deeply ingrained is the belief that colonialism is the only reason for the continent's current miseries and limited progress.

The book does not suggest that Africa forgets about its grave dark past. There is a difference between talking about and dwelling on historical grievances. The danger is dwelling on the past and so remain there, instead of moving forward. Rather than amassing self-defeating emotions about colonialism, we should cultivate a righteous anger and a conviction that history should not repeat itself.

Africans are known for being one of the most resilient peoples in the world. We counsel each other to move on when faced with challenging situations, but never done the same when it comes to colonialism. We do not talk about colonialism in order to learn from the past and help reshape historical structures to reflect the realities of the present. We talk about it with the pain and pangs of neglect and despair. We talk about it as a complaint and a reason for not making progress, and so colonialism remains our major excuse for Africa's paltry progress.

The first time I had the opportunity to visit America, I was fortunate to visit the National Air and Space Museum in Washington DC. The museum details the history of the first airplanes and displays historic aircrafts, which include the 1903 Wright Flyer as well as the Apollo 11 command module, which is the only component of the lunar mission spacecraft to return to Earth. Various other displays show how America shaped history through scientific discoveries and ingenuity.

There are many such museums around their country. The Kennedy Space Center has comprehensive displays of the various missions to space, including the Atlantis space shuttle that orbited the earth a total of 4848 times, covering nearly 203 million kilometres. The exhibits are mind-bending, but what is even more striking are the crowds of visitors. It was heartwarming to see the number of children that visit daily. These youngsters, from childhood, see great possibilities and a history full of discoveries, risk-taking and achievement. To them, life is full of possibilities, and it is the smart and courageous who turn possibility into reality.

What do we show our children? We show our children historical sites that display how we were conquered through the slave trade and how miserably we were oppressed and failed by colonialism. Make no mistake, this history is part of us and should not be done away. However, in many cases, we display these sites as though they represent the only noteworthy history of Africa. We rarely show how we triumphed against oppression. A picture of subjugation and despair is evoked in the minds of the young people who visit these places. We visit museums and our minds remain in the past. Where are the museums that showcase the inventions devised by our universities or technical colleges or fellow citizens? Where are the museums that depict the leadership and courage shown by pre-and post-colonial leaders in Africa?

Own poverty of thought and imagination chains us every day to an immutable past and an intangible future.

My recent experience in Cape Town speaks to this situation. I visited the South African city for a business meeting. After work, I would try, as much as possible, to meet locals and ask questions in an effort to understand the culture and dynamics of their way of life. Taxi drivers are usually my first port of call. On the way from the airport, the highway is lined with informal shack settlements or 'slams' as we call them in East Africa. 'Who lives in these shanty towns?' I asked the taxi driver en route to my hotel. He replied, 'Black people.' The answer was not it is 'low income people' who live there, it was directly the colour of the people who live there. I was not surprised as I knew South Africa was still divided unfortunately between blacks and whites.

During my time in Cape Town, I befriended another taxi driver. I would call him whenever I wanted to go out for dinner, shopping or site-seeing. Driving around the city, we saw several more 'squatter camps/slams'.

After several trips with him over some days, he took me through the shack settlement not far from where he lives. The area is full of small houses, many of them walled by iron sheets. I asked him if we could stop by his house to greet his family, but he seemed uncomfortable. I genuinely wanted to get to know his family as he was being such a good friend. The more I insisted, the faster he drove, shaking his head 'No', with a big smile. I understood he was ill at ease and so I desisted. It was startling to see the number of slums in Cape Town, one of the most advanced and famous cities in Africa.

My driver dropped me off at the mall and went on with his errands. As I was about to wind up my sightseeing and shopping, I called him to take me back to the hotel. He was dropping off another passenger, so he took some time to pick me up. When he finally arrived, he took a different route to my hotel, through an affluent-looking area. After driving for some time, I purposely asked the same question I had asked the taxi driver from the airport:

Me: This is a very good neighbourhood. Who lives here?

Driver: It is whites, my friend.

Me: What do you mean? Do you mean black people are not allowed to live in this area?

Driver: It is an area of whites, my friend. Only one or two black people would live in this area.

Me: What do you mean, where do blacks live then?

Driver: Mostly in the shacks and in neighbourhoods not as good as these.

Me: (sigh) Why?

Driver: It is historical. Because of apartheid.

Me: Apartheid? But that ended and people should live freely now?

Driver: It is systemic. For example, if you get a job in this company, (pointing to a signboard), you will be paid differently from the white person. The white person will be paid more.

Me: That is strange. So if you are both painters – a white and a black person – you will be paid differently?

Driver: Yes.

Me: Aw! Are you sure?

Driver: Yes.

After a moment of contemplation, I continued:

Me: If you are hired as a taxi driver like you, surely earnings would be the same, right?

Driver: No, it is different.

Me: No. It can't be. What about if both of you are Uber drivers? The rate is the same, correct?

Driver: Yes.

Me: Now, if Uber drivers earn the same, where would the white Uber driver be living?

Driver: (smiling) He would be living in this area

Me: Why then would you or another black Uber driver not live in this area?

Driver: (laughing and smiling) Yoh, it is different and difficult my friend. They end up with more money than us and we have a lot to take care of with our money, yooh.

Me: Why do they end up with more money than you? Do they work longer hours? What happens?

Driver: Oooh, actually they work fewer hours. They work from 6am to 6pm or, at the latest, 8pm and then go home. They are much more disciplined compared to us, bra.

Me: What about you, how many hours do you work?

Driver: Yoh, we work long hours, bra. Many of us work from 6am – or sometimes earlier – to midnight.

Me: So, why do you say they make more money than you then?

Driver: (laughing loudly) You see, most of the time, we do not work all the hours. We sometimes go to greet a friend and things like that. Life should be easy, bra. Also, our money is never enough because we have so many needs.

Me: Which special needs are these?

Driver: (laughing) That is a very tricky question. We have a lot of people depending on us, but also, in the evening, you must drink a bit and have someone to enjoy life with.

Me: So, the difference between you and a white Uber driver might be how you spend what you get? Right? (Both laughing profusely)

Driver: You are very smart.

Me: We need to talk about how you can live around these areas. (pointing to the suburbs we were passing through)

Driver: (laughing) Yoh, bra, you have really caught me.

Talk turned to how we could transform our lives, and I briefly became a 'a life coach' until we reached the hotel. It had been an enlightening conversation. I promised to check in on him if I happened to visit Cape Town again.

Apartheid ravaged people's lives and destroyed their hopes and dreams. However, holding on to history and using it to justify all the bad around us does not help. While South Africans now have a better chance to change the trajectory of the past – and the present – the taxi driver's mindset does not favour him. To him, he lives in a shack because of a history of apartheid and racism, irrespective of how much he earns, and how he spends it.

We hand over our destinies to someone else by blaming everybody else instead of ourselves. To those who would disagree, what then is the problem? Why is the continent not making enough progress? There are those who will even challenge the word 'enough' used here and say it is a Western measure and that the continent does not have to comply to such Western measures. Such a mindset can only keep the continent marking time, treading water not making waves. It is true that changes need to be made to address some of the challenges black South Africans face. However, the destiny of the people of the continent does not lie in its history, be it colonialism or apartheid. The destiny of the continent is squarly in the hands of Africans.

We need to change our mindsets like Ghanaian President Nana Addo Dankwa Akufo-Addo who said during the General Assembly high-level dialogue on financing for development in September 2019, that he envisioned to build 'a Ghana beyond aid' that is a 'country which has discarded a mindset of dependency, charity and handouts, and chartered a path of self-reliance for its progress and prosperity, grounded on an intelligent, disciplined use of its considerable human and material resources. Even with the best will in the world, and the most charitable governments in place, so-called donor countries', 'there will never be enough aid to develop Ghana, let alone Africa, to the level we want,' he said.[145]

Figure 3.1: Vicious cycle of blaming others and dependence

Blame and dependence
Not taking responsibility and takes no action as nothing is a result of oneself, above all, someone else will come to the rescue-dependence
Poverty as result of no/little action, and waiting for others to change our environments
No/limited progress as no action is taken to change things, above all, get supported under donor's terms

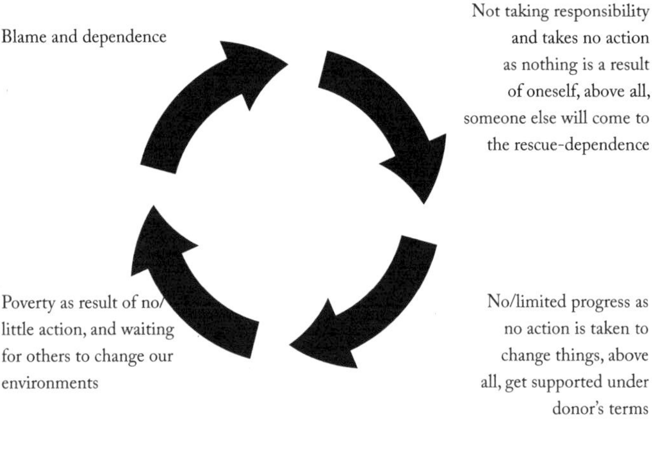

Source: Author's own

4

Vicious cycle no 4: Getting used to problems and settling for less

ALL THE NATIONS ON earth have problems or challenges that go deep into history. However, developed countries face different problems from those they faced in the past. For many parts of Africa and specifically in Sub-Saharan Africa, it has been a different story altogether. The journey of the first African leaders in the 1960s still resonates with the current journey of the larger part of the continent.

In December 1961, in his Independence message to TANU, then a political party that led the country into independence, the founding father of Tanzania, Mwalimu Julius Nyerere, identified three 'enemies' of 'development, namely, poverty, ignorance, and diseases', which needed to be 'overcome', describing them as the 'true enemies of our people'.

The reality was not much different in many other African countries at the time, many of whom were also attaining independence. Poverty, ignorance and diseases were main experiences of the time across the continent.[146] Full of hopes for new dawn and new era, pragmatic leaders of the time, Kwame Nkrumah, Mwalimu Nyerere, Jomo Kenyatta, Keneth Kaunda, Sekou Tuore, Haile Selassie just to mention a few, rallied their countrymen and women on a journey to create life free from poverty, ignorance and deceases among other enemies.

In the December 1961 address, Mwalimu Nyerere said:

> This day has dawned because of the people of Tanganyika have worked together in unity… all the time that TANU has been campaigning for Uhuru we have based our struggle on our belief in the equality and dignity of all mankind and on the Declaration of Human Rights… Yet we know that on 9th December we shall not have achieved these objects. Poverty, ignorance and diseases must be overcome before we can really establish in this country the sort of society we have been dreaming of. These obstacles are not small ones, they are more difficult to overcome than any alien government. From now on we are fighting not man but nature.[147]

The determination to eradicate poverty, ignorance and diseases for all was a seed that was going to bear socialism-Ujamaa ideology in Tanzania. Under Ujamaa, wealth distribution was supposed to be equal. Socio-economic class was against the norm and was against the law. To Mwalimu Nyerere and his likes, the fight against these 'enemies' was 'a real war'.

'I know there are still a few people who think we are joking when they hear us using the word "war". Let me assure them that were not….every year thousands of our children die needlessly for no other reason than a lack of proper care born of ignorance,' said Mwalimu Julius Kambarage Nyerere.[148]

The ambitions were supported by the first five-year plan (1964-1969), which articulated among other things, the focus areas and plans to alleviate poverty. The plan included re-invigorating agriculture with ambitions to create modern farmers, using machinery and irrigation. Also it involved expanding estates.

'.. But as well as indigenous farmers, we have in Tanganyika a number of privately owned estates and plantations. They occupy a tiny percentage of our land-less than 1% but at present they account for some 40% of the value of exports. These estates have both the capital and the technicians needed to increase output and we need an increase from them. The Government will give the estates more land if they need it.'[149]

It was a full-fledged plan, with drives for industrialisation as well. It is interesting to note what Mwalimu Nyerere had to say on industry then.

'At present we import more than 80% of the consumer goods we buy, that is excluding food. Not only that, we export our sisal and then import ropes and mats made with it; we export our cotton and import cloth; we export our coffee beans and buy tinned coffee from abroad. We buy shoes, biscuits, and enamel ware from other countries, having first exported some of the basic elements of these goods. We must remedy this state of affairs. In the next five years it is intended to greatly to speed up industrialisation and we are aiming at a rate of growth of the industrial sector which is more than twice as fast as that of agriculture. Massive investment in manufacturing is called for under the plan; we shall start to produce the consumer goods for our domestic market.'

This was a plan put in place immediately after independence. However, it sounds like a development plan speech given in the 2020s and not the 1960s. These ambitions were not unique to Tanzania. Kwame Nkrumah had spearheaded the first development plan for Ghana in 1959 to 1964 and a comprehensive seven-year plan immediately thereafter. Across the continent, the fight and strong push in the 1960s was not only focused on political independence, but also independence from poverty.

The sad part of these reflections is that more than half-a-century later, the continent is still grumbling about and grappling with the same enemies that Mwalimu Nyerere and other first African leaders highlighted and fiercely fought against in early 1960s. In many African countries, the three enemies have intensified and become even more brutal.

The continent still faces the same problems it faced at the time of most of its countries' independences, while new problems have emerged over time. The World Economic Forum lists five biggest risks facing Sub-Saharan Africa:[150]

1. Unemployment and underemployment, coupled with unskilled and low-skilled jobs;
2. Under-investment in infrastructure, with impediment of productivity of around 40% according to the World Bank;
3. Fiscal crises, with 40% of the sub-Saharan countries at risk of slipping into major debt crisis;
4. Political change, and I would attach ravaging conflicts on this point;
5. Climate change, with nine out of ten of the world's most vulnerable countries being in Sub-Saharan Africa.

Majority of the problems are similar to the problems literally faced 60 years ago, with new challenges like climate change surfacing.

Why is illiteracy still a problem in many African countries 60 years down the line? What happened with the Five-Year plans, the Ten-Year plans and the Twenty-Year plans we have had all along? For the last 65 years, the global literacy rate has been increasing by around 4% for every five years.[151] Literacy rate in Sub-Saharan Africa on the other hand has been increasing at around 2% for every five year from 1985[152]-which is half of the world pace. Some countries like Niger and South Sudan still have their literacy levels below 40% meaning more than 60% of their people cannot read and write.[153] Doesn't Africa want to shoot for the stars? We are satisfied as long as we are making 'some' progress relative to our neighbouring or fellow African countries. We are either stuck, or we have settled to the small pace of things and we are okay with it.

The minute it feels it is okay to have schools without desks or with one, two or three teachers, without enough toilets, not even the pit latrines that the community can organise to dig, then the poverty will not be because of the colour of skin but will remain in us. These are basic things for a school. This does not even refer to schools having proper laboratories, libraries and computers – that would be a next level for the continent – however; the discussion is about absence of pit latrines (the ones people dig on the ground and cover on top with timber or cement). The more the continent 'accommodates' and put up with these appalling environments, the ages it will take to come out of poverty. Unfortunately, this is not upon government only, which certainly has the biggest role to play; however, if mindset of individuals and communities do not change then things will not change fast enough.

In city suburbs, towns and rural areas, roads riddled with potholes are ubiquitous throughout the continent but we complain rather than seek solutions. We buy four-wheel drives to solve the problem of bad roads. One of the justifications of buying 4x4 cars in Africa is because of bad roads – although many such vehicle owners live and drive mostly in areas with good roads. Unfortunately, this justification is voiced mostly by governments, which have a primary role to play in building roads. Having solved the problem with high-clearance vehicles and four-wheel drives, why would government work to improve the road network?

Unstable electricity and load scheduling is another problem that has shamefully become part of life and somehow people have normalised with it. There are parts of the continent where residents wonder if electricity can be supplied for the whole day without blackouts. In other countries, a week or a month without power rationing or unscheduled blackouts is unusual. People have become accustomed to erratic power supply, it is part of life and so it is okay. A report by Moussa P. Blimpo and Malcolm Cosgrove-Davies on electricity access in Sub-Saharan Africa[154] indicates that more than half of the people connected to electricity in several countries reported to have had no electricity more than 50% of the time. On top of the less connectivity and less reliability, the report confirms that the cost of electricity in Africa is the highest in the world.

While significant progress is being made to change the trajectory, Africa still lags behind; for example India connected 100 million people to electricity in 2018, compared to just 20 million achieved in the whole of Africa.[155] More than two-thirds of the world population without access to electricity are based in Sub-Saharan Africa according to the same McKinsey article.[156]

I was left with my mouth hanging open when a Canadian friend, who was in his mid-30s then, told me that he had never experienced a power cut in his country since he was a child. The continent is significantly behind in connecting communities to electricity but even those connected don't have power for significant part of the time and still pay the highest rates in the world.

The above report goes further to say that countries in Africa could increase tax revenues by more than 4% per year solely by resolving issues related to the reliability of electricity. We are probably contented with the 'progress' we have made as long as we beat the neighbouring country or fellow African country. This is settling for less! One of the things I would commend the late President Magufuli of Tanzania for, is when he came to power, there were significant electric power stability and increase in reliability without immediate increased power supply capacity. He did not tolerate excuses for power outages – at least in the major cities. This is probably the level of 'anger' the continent may need to have to make progress.

Many still take water as a privileged commodity or far below a basic need when others think water as a scarce resource for investment. Unsafe water contribute to 6% of deaths in low-income countries.[157] It is impossible to power and roll the continent forward without water. Expand the thinking to envision making water available to lift and change trajectory of agriculture in the continent, pushing for availability to boost and expand the industrial and construction sectors, improve healthcare and education. Water plays a central role in reaching these heights. Unfortunately, the continent is still stuck in thinking about 'drinking' water, which is not even available to the majority of the people, who often walk long distances in search of it. Water projects should be commercial projects and not merely for drinking purposes.

When the community as a whole feels it is acceptable to walk several kilometres to fetch water, then we have lost the plot. We may say that it is unacceptable and nobody likes it, but if we don't develop 'anger' and 'hate' for this situation, then it will take ages to bring about the change the continent needs to have. Even unlimited donor funding will not help in the face of complacency and readiness to accommodate the problems. If we never say, 'Enough is enough', it will take generations to change the status quo.

Same applies to public health facilities in most African countries. First of all, there are not enough healthcare facilities. In the rural areas, the scarcity of facilities is worse with some people having to travel hundreds of miles to access healthcare services. Unfortunately many of these facilities do not have many of the necessities. From a shortage of basic diagnostic tools to other basic healthcare needs such as water and electricity on top of limited or too few doctors and nurses. In some cases, pregnant women have to carry gloves and sanitary pads when they go to hospital for delivery. While governments have taken a number of initiatives to improve the situation, we don't fully implement many of our own plans to address these challenges.

In 2001, Nigeria and other African Union member countries met and agreed to spend at least 15% of their fiscal budgets on healthcare[158] in order bring the continent's healthcare system into good standard. However, by 2020 Nigeria was still spending less than 5% of its federal budget on healthcare. Despite the fact that the size of the budget has increased in absolute terms, healthcare needs have skyrocketed, not only in Nigeria but around the continent, as a result of population growth and serious underfunding, coupled with continuous dependence on foreign donations.

Thank God the initial impact of the coronavirus in Africa was not as severe as many had predicted. Ten African countries had no any ventilators and 41 of the continent's countries had few than 2,000 working ventilators according to the World Health Organization.[159]

The continent has had malaria for decades. Of the 229 million cases of Malaria in the world in 2019, Africa accounted for 94% of the cases and deaths in the same year according to the

World Health Organization.[160] In 2019 alone, around 409,000 deaths were recorded from malaria in the world. This means, around 384,000 deaths of malaria were from the continent. This was more than twice as much as Covid-19-related deaths registered in the continent in a span of a year. Nigeria and the DRC account for about 34% of the global malaria deaths.[161]

These dire circumstances are a reality even after 15 years of Millennium Development Goals 4, 5 and 6, which touched healthcare and almost six years into Strategic Development Goals 3 on health and wellbeing.

We still have curable diseases claiming lives across the continent and yet, the continent sets aside the lowest research and development budget as percentage of its GDP across the global.[162] Donors fund research for us; donors share results with us; donors fund projects to implement and address the problems for us and, more often than not, the only part we probably play a significant role is saying, 'They have their own agenda'.

Admittedly, some donors may have their own agenda, but most of them, are moved by compassion and good intentions. We thank them for their partnerships but we need to invest and be at the forefront in looking for solutions for these problems. It is as if some problems are left to donors and international community for resolutions; otherwise we will live with them forever. We can never conquer our health system problems if our willingness to accommodate and live with the problems is greater than our 'dissatisfaction' and determination to eradicate them.

For more than a decade, the world has gone from one crisis to another with geopolitical shifts and turns that have seen significant changes in focus and attention of both businesses and governments. From the economic recession of 2008 to the violent extremism of the Islamic State (ISIS), the collapse in oil prices, Brexit and Covid-19, the world has not breathed freely for some time. With such challenges facing governments and especially donor countries, leaving such key sectors as public health largely at the mercy of donors is merely leaving the sector to fail.

With good determination, focus and support, the continent can rise up. The continent is not different from other continents.

The world witnessed how scientists and medical professionals around the world sprang into action to find effective medicines and vaccines after the outbreak of coronavirus. Though Africa played a 'wait and see' role at the beginning of the outbreak, it was encouraging to see several African countries coming up with their own remedies after a few months of the outbreak, the likes of Madagascar Covid Organics and other herbs concoctions used in other countries. Such medicines were yet to be approved by the World Health Organisation, but at least the efforts were made.

Makerere University in Uganda made a low-cost ventilator with locally sourced components. According to Uganda's *Daily Monitor* newspaper, the equipment was to be sold at US$3,000 per ventilator compared to US$25,000 for the imported ones.[163] Imagine, what would happen if the same sense of determination drove efforts to fight other diseases that are rampant on the continent? Unfortunately no vaccine was developed in Africa, two years after Covid-19 raged.

The problems facing the African continent are known problems and that other nations and societies have overcome for many years. These are basic problems and not mysteries. From the lack of clean and safe water to problems of bad roads full of potholes, poor schooling systems and environment, to lack of enough health facilities and medical practitioners. Problems of known diseases like malaria, tuberculosis and cholera to problems of lack of electricity and electricity reliability. The continent holds the world record for almost all problems, yet we blame the West for painting a bad picture of the continent.

We brag ourselves as resilient people as a sign that of being used to problems. I recently visited a machine store which sells different semi-industrial to household working machines and tools. In the store I saw an electric wheelbarrow. One just needs to charge and put a load in it, press a button and it is ready to move. One guides it by the tholding handles. As I was admiring it, chatting with the sales person, one person said, 'For us Africans, we brag that we can carry 100kg bag full of cereals or two or three bags of 50kg cement at once instead of working on solution to ease our work.' He went further alleging that 'we like to use physical body power more than our brain power.' I did not like the last part of the comment but pictures of young men carrying large loads in different local markets immediately came through my mind. Reality hit home.

When Covid-19 hit the world, many Africans bragged that it would not affect us because we live in harsher conditions and are used to diseases. It might be true that living in these conditions might have helped improve immunity in the continent, but it is not something we should be proud of –being used to diseases. As small as it may have been seen, it shows how complacent and okay we could be to live with diseases. Being accustomed to disease is not something we should be proud about. If we have accepted that disease is an inevitable part of our lives, why should we aggressively look for solutions?

I grew up in a village, and those who walked tens of kilometres going to the market or collecting firewood in the forest were seen as hard-working heroes. No one tried to find a way to ease the toil, but instead venerated the hard labour. Rest assured, I was not the lazy one but I remember, at the age of 12 or 13, I tried to design a water-delivery mechanism/system that would assist me to fetch water from the river while sitting at home. The initiative didn't work out, but it originated from a 'hunger' for change. Lives of people and communities will not improve without the hunger for change. Our great-grandparents fetched water with buckets from the river, our grandparents did the same, our parents did the same thing and we did the same thing and have our kids do the same thing! This is not curse, it is accommodation of the problems and have settled for less.

Public transports are cramped up and we appear okay with it and almost not having permanent solution to it. If a solution is found, then its implementation goes by snail's pace or take ages to the extent that the solutions become outpaced with new realities.

We praise ourselves as a resilient people for living under such harsh conditions, coming to terms with our impoverishment by putting a positive spin on it. While this approach may be psychologically healthy in the short term, it does nothing to change the pitiless circumstances. From those living in tin shacks in South Africa, to *fundis* (masons) or mechanics who work under tough conditions in several parts of Africa while bragging to be strong and tough; we are partners of the stone age; partners of an unknown tomorrow.

We have created and adopted the saying 'there is no hurry in Africa' and happily live with it. We continually lower our standards and find ways to justify our failures.

Other nations do not settle for less. The Japanese are a good example. In mid-November 2017, the Tsukuba Express train, which links Tokyo and the capital's northern suburbs, left the Minami Nagareyama Station at 09:44:20 instead of 09:44:40, just 20 seconds earlier. Though there were few complaints, the train operating company released a statement. 'We deeply apologise for causing tremendous nuisance to customers,' part of the press release read.

The Japanese set a high standard for themselves. For them, precision and working to improve is their daily life and culture. The train was scheduled to leave at 09:44:40. I wondered, why not 09:45 at least? Most would not split hairs and agree that if it left at 09:44. However, to the Japanese, it left exactly 20 seconds earlier and thus an apology was warranted. They hold themselves to the highest levels of responsibility and accountability. Imagine the levels of service in their banks or public offices or hospitals.

Some of the inter-city or inter-regional buses in African countries depart up to two hours or even more after time of departure indicated on the ticket and we would be okay with it. The problems are within, not on the skin.

When can we start working to solve future problems if we lag behind so much in resolving basic problems? Other countries are working to solve the problem of road congestion by working on flying cars.

Elon Musk, who was born in South Africa and moved to the USA, is anticipating future challenges that many people in the world are yet to think about. Though he was born in Africa, he is not thinking about impassable roads and electricity deficits or load scheduling. He is thinking about taking people to Mars and providing solutions for problems that are not yet problems. Companies are scrapping physical data servers to building storage space in the 'space'-cloud.

If a significant part of the continent is still throttled by basic problems of current realities, how can we confront the challenges to come, of which we may as yet be unaware until they are unlocked by discoveries, inventions, improvements and advancements? We are still shaping history, while others are shaping the future.

In many parts of the continent, corruption is seen as an accepted way of life and not a problem.

The 'Come back tomorrow' syndrome is consuming Africa.

Visit any government office for something – say, a title deed for your land, for example. Because of bureaucracy, exhaustion will likely set in before you have the document in your hands. It takes up to more than a year-and-sometimes several years to get title deed of a plot in some countries. A file would take three to five months with one person and it would feel completely okay. What about the person who would not follow up completely? It will definitely take much more time to process and get it. The impact of this is a slowdown of investments, financing/ credit processing which in turn will have multiple implication on the economy.

It is a properly coiled and complex vicious cycle! Families do not have clean water for drinking or sanitation. The same families live on less than US$2 a day, earned under severe hard environment, many of them eating only one daily meal. Such living conditions are bound to impact on health. The same families would have multiple dependents that they are unable to adequately provide for. Should any family member get sick, they may have to travel many kilometres for treatment, where they are likely to find a health facility that does not have the necessary medics or equipment and with limited medical personnel. Thus, the vicious cycle turns, swiftly and continuously, and life goes on.

We must hate these situations and circumstances at all cost. Whether it would require to be taught in schools or preached in churches and mosques, we will need to do it. The continent needs to embrace technology wholeheartedly and use it with speed. We need to cultivate for creativity and unleash our ingenuity. We must build merit, performance based and responsible societies. We must not hate to be called out as last in everything, rather we must hate to be last in everything. We are not different. The continent can only be as good as what is within us.

Figure 4.1: Vicious cycle of getting used to problems and settling for less

Not bothered/being used to the problem: bad roads, unstable or no electricity, unequipped hospitals, schools in bad shape etc. Setting low standards of ourselves
Complacence, taking no action or very slow action, if any.
Poverty with no or limited progress. After all, one is kind of confortable with the environment

Source: Author's own

5

Vicious cycle no 5: Self-defeating practices, attitudes, behaviours and culture

THE OPPORTUNITIES DENIED to ourselves and our economies stem from mismanagement, lack of integrity and trust. Over time the continent has also embraced practices that prove to be self-defeating. These are mostly soft parts of us that will require a long-term campaign to change. They can be addressed partly by incorporating some elements in the educational system; however, it is a multi-facetted quagmire. The issues need to be addressed from family level, to religious gathering as well as meeting halls and conferences, to our songs and movies. These are deep-rooted practices and way of life that hold us back from progressing faster. It is poverty within!

A culture of mistrust

Many years ago, I had a friend who was a senior government official in his country. He once told me that he did not like to travel with their national airline because he did not trust their pilots – his own qualified countrymen and women. If he had to board a plane with an African pilot, it was because he had no alternative. He had confidence in any pilot from outside the continent, but not trust in our own. This was very unfortunate to hear.

If there are two teachers – one from our own continent and another from outside the continent – we will automatically have faith in the foreign teacher more than our own teacher, not necessarily because of a disparity in knowledge or skills but rather because of an inherent bias. If you had the choice of taking your car to a mechanic and price was not a factor, would you take it to your local mechanic or to a foreign-owned Chinese workshop, for instance? A very likely reality is that many of us would take it to the Chinese mechanic. Why is this the case? An inferiority complex is at the root of this mistrust.

We do not fully trust our own teachers, nor our economists or engineers. We do not trust our own mechanics; neither do we fully trust our own doctors and nurses. We do not believe in many of the products we make. In other words, we do not trust ourselves.

In the government offices and in our homes, how many goods are made in our own countries? Whether it is furniture, fittings, or appliances, it very likely they would be imported. Does it mean no good furniture can be made in Africa? From the highest offices of the governments and private sector to lower offices, it is seldom that one finds locally made furniture and fittings. If anything, such locally made goods could only possibly be found in the local government offices or not well-established private offices. If governments do not trust their own people's work how can individuals trust them?

Let us look at trade between the European Union (EU) and Africa in 2019, for example.

' ... almost 70% of goods exported from the EU to Africa were manufactured goods ... over 65% of goods imported to the EU from Africa were primary goods.'[164]

We prefer buying imported goods to those made locally by our own people. In 2019, Africa recorded a trade deficit of almost US$60.2 billion; which is almost equivalent to the entire economy of Tanzania, which ranks ninth in the continent as of 2020.[165] The continent's deficit increased from US$58 billion in 2018 but also widened from US$15 billion in 2005.[166] This means our continent's imports have quadrupled over a period of 14 years compared to the continent's exports.

Yet, we complain about a lack of jobs and grumble about stagnant economies. Exports for Africa is key, not only because of forex or extension of market, but because of price realisation as well. With low disposable income in the continent which limits price maximisation, exports are one of the best ways for businesses in the continent to fetch better prices elsewhere, increase revenue and profitability.

How can we employ more people, especially the increasing number of young people who are jobless by mainly import trading? In Africa, the richer you become, the less it is 'expected' to buy local products. Imported goods are a matter of pride including garments. In this case a sizable portion of the funds are not paid to the businesses in the continent and hence do not circulate in the continent's banking system and economy. The practice denies both the banks and local businesses the opportunity for bigger growth. If we do not encourage buying from Africa, we will be holding back our own growth pace.

A culture of the second-rate

An important question is why we do not believe in ourselves and our products? Some may respond that our history of colonialism, apartheid, capitalism and the West are to blame because they inculcated an inferiority complex in our minds. But let us look in the mirror and ask ourselves some uncomfortable questions. What quality of work do we produce when given tender or business and timelines? What is the quality of our workmanship and finishes? If the answer is 'not of good quality', then that is not driven by colonialism, apartheid, the IMF, the World Bank nor the West.

Do we keep our promises in terms of delivery time? There are anecdotes and practices in which people take their car to a local mechanic and manufacturer's original spares are changed for fictitious spares or have working parts replaced by inferior or broken components. In several local automotive repair shops, one needs to stand there watching their cars being fixed to avoid fictitious spares put in or 'ghost' fixes claimed be done. It is a waste of time and resources. How many times must the car's bodywork be shoddily repaired before trust fails?

What about giving some of the construction work to our masons? How many masons would use the correct cement ratio if there was no one supervising them? If the answer is not many, then we have a big problem to address. Yet, we expect people to loyally support and buy their second- or third-rate goods or services. People end up importing products or services because they are not available in their own countries or if they are available, they are of inferior quality or insufficient quantity.

People are so tired of this sort of behaviour that there is a Swahili saying in Tanzania that says, '*Fundi wa kuaminiwa ni kinyozi pekee*', which means 'the only trustworthy technician/ artisan/skilled hands men/women is a barber or beauty salon person'. This means most other artisans/technicians/skilled men and women are not fully trusted as they do not delivery their promises most of the time. On the hand, barbers and salonists work on a person's hair when the person is present physically. There is no come tomorrow or the day after tomorrow.

For instance, if a local contractor is awarded a tender for road construction, what quality of road will they build?

We cannot have all the good work and projects only given to foreign contractors because 'we cannot produce quality work'. If many of the quality projects with better returns do not end up with residents/local people of the countries in the continent because of such hesitations among other things, then it will take longer to come out of the woods.

It is too easy to blame the public sector that issues these contracts. What about the rest of us? How well do we implement these projects if our tenders are successful? One of the local contractors who is a friend of mine shared his hesitation to partner with other local contractors in big projects because he is not sure whether they will deliver to the standard required. 'Some deliver the best while others deliver substandard work,' said the contractor.

These are some of the practices that hinder cooperation and working together. Do we all keep our promises or commitments? How much do we strive to deliver the best quality? Do we see the best quality roads delivered by most contractors in our localities? These are some of the questions that we need to ask ourselves and to effect change in our way of doing things from individuals, society to a nation should the answer be negative.

We cannot have most of our major infrastructure projects given to foreign contractors because we cannot produce quality work. If this does not change, it will take many years to build strong economies in which people thrive.

With some exceptions, we have challenges to produce quality goods and services; we do not keep our promises and we end up not trusting each other, which leads to us buying less or not buying at all from each other, resulting in low revenues and thus low output, which then translates into little or no investment, which, in turn, leads to continuing poor service and substandard quality products. With these self-defeating practices and behaviours, poverty continues to stick to us. The longer we take to change, the longer our self-issued license for the vicious cycle of poverty will remain valid.

First-rate goods and services do not just appear with time. Similarly, quality of life is sought for, it is created, it is fought for and it starts from inside out. In other words, we cannot live a quality life if it does not exist inside us as individuals or inside us as society or within our systems. It is what is within our education system, homes, institutions and within our workplaces that need to change to realize the best outcomes we long for.

The call for change is everyone's job. It is not governments' only. Voices must be heard and pushback must be felt from all fronts – from the governments, communities, non-governmental organisations, as well as churches, mosques and private organisations. From our favourite artists and songwriters to songs and dances in dancing halls and open spaces. We must demand best of ourselves. As a society we must move from self-defeating ways of living to build a better tomorrow for the continent.

Competition not co-operation

We seldom partner amongst ourselves for successful ventures. Why is it that foreign companies, even from different countries, can partner and work together successfully but for many of us on the continent, this is nearly an impossibility? It is easier for a local contractor to partner with a Chinese contractor than a fellow local contractor.

Most of the continent's infrastructure projects are undertaken by foreign contractors with China penning around 62% of the projects in 2018.[167] What would the impact be on African economies if 70% – or even 50% – of ongoing infrastructure work of approximately US$100 billion using 2018 mark[168] on the continent was done by African contractors? African governments fund around 42% of the continent's infrastructure,[169] however, most projects still go to foreign firms.

It is understandable that most local companies lack capacity and experience to do such projects, but what about partnering with each other? It is also understandable there is a dearth of local experience in special large engineering projects like railways, big bridges or massive dams like the Grand Renaissance Dam of Ethiopia or the Mwalimu Nyerere Dam currently under construction in Tanzania. However, what about the construction of normal roads or high-rise buildings or small to medium and large water projects?

One of the ways to address a lack of capacity and experience is for these contractors to come together and do a joint venture. What prevents our local contractors from forming even a temporary consortium to bid for these big projects? Unfortunately, this is not happening much and, if it does happen, it is at immaterial scale. If partnering within a country proves to be difficult, what about partnering across borders? What if a Zambian contractor was to partner with a Zimbabwean contractor or a Namibian or Tanzanian contractor to pool resources, skills and experience and bid for bigger and better projects?

In South Africa, Broad-Based Black Economic Empowerment (BBBEE) is government policy. This is a progressive measure put in place to help fasttrack black, Indian and coloured participation in the economy as these races were disadvantaged by apartheid. While the measure has been criticised for only enriching a few individuals and businesses, it is better than nothing.

How are non-white businesses using the opportunity to progress? Why do we not see these few black-owned successful companies and businesses expanding to the rest of Africa? As it stands, said Muzi Siyaya, who served GIBB Engineering and Architecture in South Africa as Group Business Development Executive, 'there are pockets of excellence of large black-owned companies across various sectors such as construction, engineering, legal and auditing'.[170] He asserted that it had been a significant challenge for black-owned businesses to expand outside South Africa because of lack of balance sheet and economies of scale.

What about pulling resources together? If not pulling resources together within the country, why not with other countries' businesses for bigger and better contracts or in this case expanding to the rest of the African countries? Or is it that the large black owned enterprises – LBOEs as they call them – have reached the pinnacle of success as they are much bigger that other black owned enterprises within their territories hence less incentive to expand to the rest of Africa?

It is very unfortunate that even fellow Africans' businesses in South Africa are being torched and set on fire because they think the Zimbabweans, Nigerians, Malawians, Tanzanians, Kenyans and Somalis are stealing their opportunities. They never torch any foreign-non-African owned businesses; but those of their fellow African. It does not mean they torch other foreign-owned businesses, no. Why would they even think of setting their fellow Africans' businesses on fire? It does not make them any better. These minds should emancipate and climb a ladder to see the other side of the wall and the opportunities that lie ahead of the continent. These are the practices and beliefs that must change.

Forget about the sickening xenophobic acts. What about smaller companies in South Africa partnering for bigger jobs and assignments with the advantage of BBBEE? Unfortunately, discussing these issues for South Africans invokes a race issue. It is very unfortunate that some of the already discussed self-defeating behaviours and practices are many times tied to a black race. However, if such behaviours and practices are done by any form of race, and will yield the same result, it is poverty within, not on the skin.

What prevents us from working together for the next frontier? Is it been contented with our business sizes and growth as long as we are better than the businesses around us? Or is it that we think too small or not just trusting each other or is it jealousy? Few of the local contractors I interact with generally opine that they hesitate to partner with other contractors because of integrity issues, lack of commitment, focus and divergent objectives.

It is very unfortunate we allow ourselves to be in such a state. This goes against the call of nature that weaker players should unite to play against strong players. Unfortunately, the reality facing the continent both as countries and as businesses is the opposite; the strong players unite to play against the weak and we remain blaming the IMF, the World Bank and the colonialists. This is why the African Continental Free Trade Area (AfCTA) is a critical step for the continent and should be embraced.

A study done in Tanzania and published in the International Journal of Construction Engineering and Management in 2019 lay bare some of the challenges for joint venture in the construction sector in Tanzania. 'Construction related challenges include low experience and capacity of the other partner and shoddy construction work quality by a partner(s).' They went on to conclude that '...the most challenges in contractors' contractual relationship in the joint venture in Tanzania are: poor management of money for the project by partner(s), interruption and termination of work by client, loss of trust among partners, low experience and capacity of the other partner and non-adherence to the conditions of the contract'.[171]

These issues are not unique with the construction sector or to Tanzania. Regrettably, these issues are part of our society and some of the solutions to address them must be societally based. We cannot avoid revamping our education system to inculcate right work ethics and values, having vibrant working alternative dispute resolution (ADR) systems and policy-based supports to smoothen environment of businesses working together. Partnerships and working together within and without our territories hold great potential for the continent.

Savings and Credit Co-operative Societies (SACCOS) are good examples of individuals working together for a 'bigger' cause. These are cooperative groups of people with similar interests that decide to contribute an agreed sum either for investment or a social cause. The majority of the groups are formed by women, though there are many groups formed by men as well. Kenya has one of the most vibrant cooperative groups in the continent with over 15,000 groups and more than 10 million memberships having an asset base of more than US$6 billion.[172]

Uganda, Tanzania, Nigeria and other African countries have similar groups. These are exemplary groups to help grow individual and societal income by co-investing or tackling social issues. Unfortunately, most cooperatives face similar challenges across the countries with varied magnitude. In one of the regions in Uganda, out of 453 SACCOS groups registered, 312 SACCOS, which is 69%, were struggling due to fraud and poor governance among other challenges, while 64 SACCOS, making 13%, had collapsed according to the report by Project of Financial Inclusion in Rural Areas-PROFIRA.[173]

Kenya's bigger base of cooperatives are not immune to the same challenges. 'An increasing number of Kenyan SACCOS are reeling under the weight of mismanagement, fraud and bad loans that have put the Sh1 trillion sector on a path of instability that if not reversed could have damaging contagion on the entire economy,'[174] reads part of *a Business Daily* article of 11 March 2019.

According to the article, the SACCOS savings form about 30% of all savings in Kenya and about 6% of the nominal GDP of Kenya. When these SACCOS are mismanaged and loans are not paid back, the implications would squarely be felt on the country's economy.

The impact would have been significant on poverty alleviation if most of the SACCOS were well managed. This is one of the best ways to raise capital and co-invest for the majority poor. It is all in our hands and within us.

Many foreigners living in Africa collaborate and support each other. An Israeli or Turkish, Russian or English business in Africa is in the first place supported by their fellow countrymen and women or businesses. An English person is likely to drive landrover and or own majority of things made in the United Kingdom even when lives in a different continent.

There are a few Africans who have cultivated a culture of working together, who have pushed their businesses to the next level, like Somalis outside Somalia, Nigerians outside Nigeria or white South Africans within and outside South Africa. Unfortunately, when done within a country creates the sour taste of discrimination, racism and tribalism, which should not be encouraged in the continent.

I have an Indian friend living in Tanzania, who together with his fellow Indians have several venture capital funds for investing into different business opportunities. As a group, they have been able to invest in banks, hotels and insurance companies in millions of US dollars. This friend once told me that venture capital funds are one of their best approaches to grow their businesses and owning shares in the economies. He reiterated that most of the venture capital funds are tightly managed including those co-owned by close relatives.

Flipping the picture to the continent's co-operatives and collaborations, we experience a different wave of results in many instances. From construction sectors to socio-economic groups like SACCOS, some results are not impressive as seen above. We need to develop the likes of our SACCOS groups designed to grow our middle class; forge stronger mergers and business collaborations from all business aspects and sizes for expansive and long-term breakthrough. We need to build a culture of mutual trust, respect and collaboration. It has to start from within.

Another Indian friend of mine once shared his success journey with me. He owns multiple businesses worth hundreds of million US dollars, some on his own and others as part of the family. His grandfather had built a good business which his father and uncles inherited thereafter. After his uncles and his father received their inheritance, the elder uncle persuaded the rest of the siblings to put their money together to do bigger business instead of each one of them parting ways with what they got. 'This was our breakthrough,' he said.

The elder uncle headed the business and steered it with success. From there, this friend of mine was picked to lead the businesses created to greater heights. Along the way, he also started his own businesses from the dividend shared and his remunerations. The family business grew from a few millions of dollars to hundreds of million dollars. His personal businesses blossomed as well. He is now investing with his son, who was initially working for him. His daughter-in-law supplies some raw materials to the business he co-owns with his son. He recently told me that they made a few million dollars profits in this new business with his son. This friend of mine is a third generation of their family business and already he is instilling the same investment values in his son, the fourth generation. He marked that the same practice is exercised by many Indian families and that is how they succeed.

We don't have many success stories of inheritance with many us in the continent. Many of the inherited businesses in the continent collapse or struggle within few years of been inherited. We would seldom be willing to co-invest with relatives leave alone friends. With this 'culture', it is very difficult to create wealth and long-lasting wealth.

We have a long way to go but it is not all lost. We have Nigerians at least who like to support each other especially when outside their country. The Somalis do business together and support each other, but mostly when they are outside their country. Kenyans and Egyptians are the same. Nigerians are setting the pace with some good examples. A number of Nigerian businesses are expanding not only to the rest of Africa but also outside the continent.

There are quite a number of Nigerians who are thinking big and boldly. There are Nigerian banks expanding into the continent and building guts to expand to mature markets like Europe and America. Zenith Bank, Ecobank, UBA, Access Bank Plc are all some of the examples of Nigerian banks which operate in several African countries and in Europe, China,

USA and United Arab Emirates (Dubai). There are Nigerian businesses advertising on CNN, growing their territorial influence in other continents.

This is the power of an expansive vision and unfettered zeal. This is what is needed in Africa and it is possible. The continent is a not a basket case of failed people. However, the few Nigerians doing well should only act as proof that it is possible and not make us think that we already have good representatives in this aspect and thus we have arrived or achieved it all. We need this zeal and hunger across the continent. We need businesses with great values, passion and ceiling-breaking ambitions for the next boundaries.

By the way, Nigerians are larger than life. They are physically big people; they talk and laugh loudly; they work hard; they are big on churches, mosques and witchcraft, famous con men and great businessmen. They try to do everything big. Their population is the biggest in the continent and still growing very fast, but also their economy is the largest in Africa. With these glimpses of hope, there is still enormous poverty in Nigeria. Addressing many of the things 'within' that hold us back will unleash a different Nigeria, a transformed Senegal, a distinct Tanzania, a unique Chad, an exceptional Zimbabwe and why not a thriving continent?

Tearing down, not raising up

Another self-defeating behaviour is that we do not support each other. Paul Pogba, the French footballer, is a renowned central midfielder of African descent. His transfer fee of €105 million from Juventus to Manchester United broke the world record in 2016, and remains the highest transfer fee for the English clubs to date. Yet, his own brother did not vote for him in the FIFA Ballon d'Or Award in 2016, despite the fact that Paul had been a recipient of a Golden Boy Award in 2013, a Bravo Award in 2014, and was named to the UEFA Team of the Year in 2015, as well as the FIFPro World XI after helping Juventus reach the 2015 UEFA Champions' League final, their first in 12 years. Pogba's older brother, Florentin Pogba, was a national team captain for Guinea and he used his three votes in favour of Lionel Messi, Cristiano Ronaldo and Manuel Neuer, leaving his own brother out. Perhaps Florentin was just being objective but was very unusual.

When I released my first book, *A Distant Perspective on the U.S. and Obama Administration*, I expected friends and relatives to buy the book. The contrary was true. Friends from other countries bought online and some asked for signed copies and paid for them. However, while many friends in my own country congratulated me, the majority did not buy the book but rather requested a free copy. I was not offended by such requests, and I gave out a number of free copies, but the culture seems to be different from developed countries, where friends would show their support by buying copies and even, when possible, buying copies for their friends. They support each other.

It reminds me of an example cited in the book *Capitalist Nigger* by Chika Onyeani. He alluded to a tale he had heard of a black investor who had accumulated money and built a 'high-tech, modern, sparkling supermarket' in a black neighbourhood 'either in Cleveland or Detroit' in the USA. The investor had projected a minimum revenue of US$250,000 to break even or make a small profit. Unfortunately, the business could not generate the minimum revenue while another supermarket owned by non-black investors not far from his business generated revenue of US$2 million with most customers being black folks. The black investors had to close eventually.

These issues are not unique to Africa, as the previous

anecdote makes clear. However, the magnitude, I contend, is greater. Moreover, race is not the point of the previous anecdote. Rather it shows that we, as black people, do not support our own. If the attributes, behaviours, attitudes and practices discussed in this book are evinced by any race, the results would be the same. It is not about being black or white. It is the values, behaviours and ways of life that count. It is unfortunate that the same behaviour exhibited by blacks in America, in this context, is the same behaviour displayed by many Africans on the continent. It feels bad talking about supporting each other based on the colour of the skin. It is below the bar – below the threshold of humanity. Perhaps the focus should then be on why do Africans avoid supporting other Africans?

I had a friend from Zimbabwe, who had visited Tanzania a couple of times. On one of his visits, I invited him to our church for Sunday service. He was excited to join me until I told him that we had a few Zimbabweans in our church. He immediately declined the invitation, explaining that it was likely that his fellow Zimbabweans would hit him up for help. I felt bad, not only for his comment but also because of such attitudes that define us and block us from achieving our full potential. Who is to blame? The man who refused to go to church in order to avoid meeting his fellow Zimbabweans or his countrymen and women? This is a sad reality in many parts of the continent.

One of Tanzania's most respected businessmen, the late Reginald Mengi, once said that Africans are second-class citizen in their own countries. Compared to a local investor, a foreigner would enjoy first-class treatment in public and private offices throughout the continent and earn trust and support for any investments and dealings. To the contrary, a local investor is likely to face a lot of road blocks and frustrations before they can get their way forward. What is wrong with us? Why do we not support each other? When we use the word 'support' it may connote 'favours', but why do we not treat each other the same as we would treat a foreigner, let alone support each other? Even worse, it is as though we discriminate against each other. We do not want each other to succeed.

Should we still attribute these attitudes to colonialists who divided us and made us discriminate against each other or look down on each other? Do we keep blaming the very real agents of colonialism and apartheid, thinking that some day things will change by themselves? Or do we need more time to change because these beliefs were entrenched by 'colonialism' for such a long time? We need to take charge of our own destiny and stop making these 'reality' excuses. These are soft things that can be taught in our schools in a positive way.

We also cannot work together because we cannot in many cases stand each other succeeding. We only value our own success. We may even fight each other and pull each other down rather than have one of us progressing. A friend of mine used this analogy in one of our discussions: 'If you find two Africans in a deep pit trying to get out of it, just lower down a long step ladder as if you want to help and go away, because they will not come out or will take some time to come out. Either one of them trying to go up the ladder first will be pulled down by the other person.' This is crab in the bucket mentality at its best, where the idea of 'if I cant have it, neither can you' prevails.

Take, for example, the sporadic xenophobic attacks in South Africa against other African businesses. The Zimbabweans, Somalis, Nigerians and Malawians are seen as stealing opportunities from South African citizens. Yet white foreign-owned businesses are not targeted. They cannot stand seeing their fellow black Africans succeed, yet we would not have any problems with other non-black foreign-owned businesses, including those from Africa.

We limit our own progress by our jealousy and selfishness. While jealousy and selfishness are part and parcel of being human, in Africa, such self-defeating behaviour is endemic. We pull each other down and do everything possible to block each other from progress.

There are no words for this. Jealousy coupled with nepotism and selfishness hinder us from widely sharing opportunities. We are disadvantaged in terms of education, skills, exposure and experience. We would expect a greater drive for developed countries to offer bigger and transformative scholarships, but even some of those few that are freely given out of compassion may not be fully utilised or some do not reach the intended communities.

We can complain until the end of time, but if we do not address these inhibiting factors, then we willingly keep at bay much of what is possible today. Untold success and wealth passes us by because of these artificial limitations.

Satisfied too early

Thinking that we have arrived is another self-defeating behaviour. The only comparison we have is among ourselves, and thus the few who have made progress overrate their own achievements. Whether in employment or business, such mindset never take one far. A contractor with such a mentality may not want to partner with others. In their minds, they lead in their sphere of operation and this vanity may blind them to bigger opportunities on the continent. This mentality has seen many individuals and businesses failing abruptly while others fail to break the ceiling of success because of too early satisfaction or a thinking of having made it especially when compared to others. It applies to countries as well. A lot will be left behind undone if a country feels okay and satisfied growing at, say 5% or 6% because their counterparts are growing at a slower pace, irrespective of the rate required to grow to get out of poverty. Unfortunately, we compare ourselves with the weak instead of comparing with the best. All these play a significant role in stalling progress.

Cultural constraints

A lot of the time we talk about the big issues and forget about the petty behaviours, practices and cultures that significantly affect our progress. Throughout our countries there are people who believe in witches and witchdoctors or 'traditional healers'. While some of these families cannot afford two meals a day, they would be willing to exchange their only goat just to bewitch a neighbour who has built a house. Whether witchcraft works that way or not, the energy and resources spent on such pursuits by very poor families is pitiful.

It is a widespread practice that holds the continent back. Think, for example, of a football team that believes it can win matches, not through physical skill and intense training, but by applying what Nigerians call voodoo. It is very disgraceful. From the football clubs to national teams, there is a wide belief in such practices. Such beliefs are packaged as traditional healing but, in my opinion, are rather a traditional curse in a way of progress. Healing means to make better. How then can we talk about traditional 'healing' (voodoo), when its proponents resist progress, be it in education or business, sports and prefer everybody to be equally poor or non-performer?

Some of these believers believe they do not have to invest much in customer service but still attract customers through voodoo. I wonder why these people can't do magic to invent and innovate things if they have power to attract customers irrespective. Think of any area or region in our countries that practise these beliefs. There is no progress in those areas and development is hearsay. Whether the area is in South Africa, or in Nigeria or Malawi or Tunisia or Central Africa, the results are the same – poverty.

It is true that such beliefs are held worldwide, but its practise in the continent is very big. A significant portion of Africa's population believes in such practices. An article published in *Africa Security Review* journal by the former head of Africa Institute of South Africa, Erich Leistner, asserts, 'witchcraft… clearly is a major factor retarding Africa's economic development, though its economic backwardness also plays a role'.

He continued affirming that 'considering how severely witchcraft impinges on development, it is remarkable that the subject is totally ignored in the vast literature on African development'.[175] Such people believe they can succeed in business and other aspects of life without working hard. I have worked with Nigerians, and I can attest to their passion and hardworking ethic. However, despite the zeal and passion of Nigerians, there are parts of their country that are deeply impoverished and undeveloped, due in part to such 'traditional' beliefs. Simply put, those who have succeeded or made good progress, whether in Nigeria, or in South Africa or any another country, have worked hard.

Leistner seconds further the above contemplation by asserting that 'In South Africa, as throughout Africa, many business people use the services of traditional practitioners of magic to ensure success by attracting customers, fending off competitors, and discovering favourable opportunities'. How pitiful this reality is in the 21st century. It is a poverty within!

Frivolous youth

In addition to not supporting each other, our jealousy that

compels us to drag each other down and our belief in witches and witchdoctors whose 'magic powers' can help us prosper without the necessity for hard work, we have many of our young people focusing on alcohol, partying and gambling. Many of our youth spend their time thinking about the next beer, glass of wine or local brew, or the next episode of a favourite television series. They spend their time on social media moving from one celebrity account to the other, soaking up the details of love affairs, fights and gossip. For many, this has become a significant part of their lives.

Have these young people given up on their lives or do they hold the illusion that some day, somehow, life will correct itself miraculously? The idle mind is a workshop for the devil. Others call it a time bomb. The young people have chosen to settle for less than they deserve.

To understand the magnitude of this, just reflect on the young people in the cities and, even more so, those in the villages. It is scary. How is the continent going to utilise these people? How are they going to contribute to the welfare and progress of their nations? Are they going to be an asset to their communities and countries or a liability? Many of them may long to make strides and progress in life but, at the same time, they do nothing to better themselves, and worst of all, they engage in activities and behaviours that deepen their problems and push them into yet more poverty. It is indeed a vicious cycle that comes from what is within us!.

Look at who has the most following on social media in the continent. Not the most successful businessmen or women in the continent. Not even the most decorated CEOs of successful companies in Africa. Of course, not even politicians. It is largely musicians, movie and TV personalities, sports stars and comedians. Nothing wrong about this at all, however, these are the groups that hundreds of millions of young people in the continent gather their insights from. In many instances these are the trendsetters and shapers of weighty part of the youth conversations and lives in the continent. Their impact is felt across corners and walls of many meeting ups. From the concrete walls of universities and colleges to the chats and catch-ups in barber shops and beauty parlours, the influence of these groups is significant.

For example, 30-year-old Nigerian singer-songwriter David Adedeji Adeleke – better known as Davido – had a following of over 20 million people at the beginning of 2021 while fellow Nigerian Ali Dangote, the richest person on the continent, had yet to reach 1 million followers on any of his social media platforms at that time. This is a trend across the continent. Only the Zimbabwean billionaire Strive Masiyiwa, who has an audience of around 5 million who follow his motivational messages on Facebook, comes close. It is hard to find any other successful business mogul or CEO that has a following of more than 3 million people. No wonder a good number of young people in barber shops and in informal groups have write-ups of songs and some good thoughts of movie scripts, mostly on love affairs, but rarely do they have other business plans.

It is the age of technology, and many young people on the continent who spend a generous amount of time on these platforms are not necessarily connecting to the minds that are shaping economies, whether in policies or in actions. The majority of our young people are ill-equipped to talk about the economy, businesses, investments, partnership, the ICT revolution, values and ethics. We are the sum of our daily conversations and thoughts, which lead to action. Probably the burden is on those who shape economies as well – policy-makers, investors and successful businesses. Their conversation may not be connecting to young people.

During the Youth Employment in Agriculture conference in Kigali in August 2018, a young lady urged the policy-makers and supporting organisations to 'make agriculture sexy' in order to attract youth. These comments generated a lot discussions across many platforms, however, what she was communicating was that the current agriculture set up does not squarely talk to young people. The question would be how many things we would need to make 'sexy' for youths to come on board. Is it just a disconnection of generations or what is within the young people? We cannot blame the youth. It is their space. All of us, young and old alike, need to create a convergence zone. Can our singers sing on agriculture or a bit about business or economy, for instance?

Spurred by the disruption caused by the coronavirus pandemic, businesses have woken up to the reality of where people spend most of their time. Many businesses are strategising on how to capitalise on these social media and online platforms, establishing new distribution channels focused on reaching out online. The trend is likely to help contribute to re-shaping young people's participation in economies. This could be a blessing in disguise.

The question remains: what is going to dominate the continent young people's conversations and thoughts in the short term and longer term – love, alcohol or celebrity gossip? What are young people in China, India and Singapore thinking about? What about in other continents? The forces of nature and time can course correct these trends. However, we cannot afford to leave it all on nature and time to shape the future of the continent. Certainly, other continents are not leaving it all to nature and time, they are shaping it.

We are a community with different lifestyles and thus, in no way is it expected that everyone will think the same way. However, if our daily discourse is mainly dominated by who can drink more, and which celebrity has posted which pictures or gossip, then from that we will reap. We cannot harvest maize when we planted sorghum – although they do look alike when growing.

These are difficult conversations. However, if we do not have enough of these robust debates to help shape such trends and practices, the longer we will have to endure our current circumstances and low level of progress.

Integrity deficit

We are talking about self-defeating cultures. What about important values such as integrity, honesty, discipline and trustworthiness? How do we as a continent fare in these values, with regard to individuals, business community and politicians?

Warren Buffet, one of the richest people on the planet, once said: 'We look for three things when we hire people. We look for intelligence, we look for initiative or energy, and we look for integrity. And if they don't have the latter, the first two will kill you, because if you're going to get someone without integrity, you want them lazy and dumb.'[176]

However intelligent we may consider ourselves to be, and however determined and energised, we can never register long-lasting successes without integrity and honesty. This applies to individuals, organisations, communities and nations. Well-known American self-help author Napoleon Hill had this to say: 'When you are able to maintain your own highest standards of integrity, regardless of what others may do, you are destined for greatness.'[177]

Another American author and motivational speaker, Zig Ziglar, echoed this sentiment: 'Honesty and integrity are absolutely essential for success in life – all areas of life. The really good news is that anyone can develop both honesty and integrity.'[178]

In other words, one can seldom talk about greatness or true success or development without these fundamental values. The level of integrity, discipline and honesty determines the level of development in a society. It is not the other way round. Integrity, discipline and honesty must be present before development can get off the ground.

In Africa, we tend to focus on these important values mainly when it comes to politicians. However, even politicians come from the same communities in which we live. They are products of our communities and largely represent who we are as a people.

Integrity, discipline and honesty play a significant role in our African context of mistrust and unwillingness to work together for the greater good. Gaps of integrity, discipline and honesty are killing many opportunities in Africa. A lack of moral values has far-reaching and incalculable consequences. Many businesses in Africa fail to get off the ground because of a lack of suitable management. There are so many businesses that have not been opened in Africa because one could not get the right person to run it. Some people have stopped or significantly delayed investing in businesses of all kinds because they cannot find someone trustworthy enough to run them. These are all opportunities lost that could help stimulate the economy and employ more young people.

I know a number of friends and colleagues' businesses that failed as a results of mismanagement and squandering by relatives or friends. Also, a good number of those who borrowed money from friends or relatives to start businesses have never returned it. As a result of these gaps, many are hesitant to invest and tend be overcautious to lend/support to their relatives and friends.

All these affect small and medium enterprises' growth and hence affect our economies. To the contrary, businesses need to boom for the continent to flourish. Africa is dependent on SMEs. Nigeria is the largest economy on the continent but 90% of its businesses are small, medium and micro enterprises (SMMEs), according to the Presidential Enabling Business Environment Council (PEBEC), a Nigerian council that was formed in 2016 to work on improving the ease of doing business in the country.[179]

With limited formal employment in Africa, many people start their own businesses from necessity, be it a salon or barbershop, a coffee shop or a brickyard. A taxi or a motorbike offers small business opportunities. In 2015, Uganda, Angola, Cameroon and Botswana had the most entrepreneurs per capita in Africa according to a report entitled 'Entrepreneurship around the World', released by a UK-based B2B products and service directory, Approved Index.[180] At the same time, Uganda, Angola and Malawi are reported to be the leading countries with highest rate of business failure in Africa.[181]

In South Africa, for example, some 70% of emerging small businesses fail within their first two years of operation, according to Chris Darrol, CEO of the Small Business Project (SBP).[182]

Many of them deteriorate and some collapse because of mismanagement. Reasons range from cashflow problems, poor planning and management, wanting to do it alone, lack of business knowledge, skills and infrastructure as well as limited access to finance among other reasons.

From hawking and roadside selling, to pubs and boutiques to medium-size businesses such as small manufacturing facilities or small chain stores or supermarkets – all of these rein in the hearts of many African economies and especially in Sub-Saharan Africa. These are businesses that require minimal amounts of capital – from as little as US$50 to millions of dollars with the majority of businesses somewhere in between. The vicious cycle of poverty kicks in here.

There are a number of young people who are desperately looking for seed capital to start a small business, but they cannot find anyone to finance them because of a lack of trust, fueled by integrity and honesty issues. There are a number of people – especially young people – looking for a car to become an Uber driver to sustain themselves and their families. There are many people who could fund them but they would not invest in Uber because of doubts about the integrity of the drivers. This means a wasted opportunity for employment, a missed opportunity for earning, loss of government revenue and a lost opportunity for the economy.

There are young people looking in vain for a US$50 or US$100 or US$500 loan to start a business while there are plenty of individuals – let alone institutions – that could lend the money – and here does not refer to rich individuals, no – a middle-class person could offer the loan.

Many loan opportunities are not realised because the lenders think they will not get back their money. This happens at individual and community levels. Such reluctance to part with the money gives the lie to the continent-wide spirit of *ubuntu* – as South Africans call it, which is derived from the Zulu saying *Umuntu ngumuntu ngabantu*, 'I am, because you are'.

The entrepreneurial ideas that could be realised within a capital range of US$500 to US$100,000[183] could well be a permanent solution for Africa's widespread unemployment – a revolutionary force that could steadily change the continent. For small businesses across the continent, the size of these loans are typical, and are commonly sourced from individuals or savings and credit groups or formal financial institutions.

Joseph is a friend who has had bad experience giving several loans to relatives, friends and a few young people, most of which were not returned. He has vowed since then not give further loans; rather, he would support them with no strings attached to avoid quarrels and broken friendships. There have been countless such bad experiences with many people I know.

I have had several such experiences, too. I was driving back from work one Monday. At a traffic junction, a roadside bookseller came to my car's window holding a bundle of books that he was trying to sell to me. I lowered the car's window, greeted him and asked his name. I told him I was not going to buy a book, rather I would want to offer him books to sell at a big discount and that I would collect the money only after he had sold them. Depending on his success, I would offer him more stock to distribute to his fellow roadside booksellers and I would talk to a few other authors to give him some credit stock for distribution as well. He was very happy with the proposal and indicated he was ready to start execution immediately or when I was ready. I told him I was ready to start and asked him to wait for me on the other side of the junction.

In the car, I had several copies of my first book. After crossing the traffic lights, I handed him 10 copies and took his phone number after agreeing on a selling price, his discount then I drove off. After almost a week, I met him. He had only three books remaining as he had sold seven copies. When I asked about the money, he told me he had family issues, which forced him to use the money. I told him it was not a good practise to mix business and personal issues. I spent few minutes to tell him to always protects his capital and other people's money, and try as much as possible to separate personal issues from business. After the 'lecture', I again handed over seven books to bring his stock back to ten books. I reminded him of the bigger picture of becoming distribution agent for the road booksellers and that it was important to keep discipline and trustworthiness.

Unfortunately, after taking the books he disappeared for almost six months, with his phone not reachable. The last time I saw him, he walked away pretending to have not seen me and disappeared. This was a low-value credit/support to give to someone whom I did not know very well. However, his dishonesty deprived him a bigger opportunity. There are several other bigger examples of such practices. If a community would have 100 or 1000 or one million of such people, then much bigger business conversations stall hence a poverty within. I have personally lost money several times in almost similar fashion. Some of my friends and people I know have lost much larger amounts in similar circumstances too. I cannot recall a friend who has never lost money and never had to terminate a business venture. If half of these small investments worked, they would have contributed to sizable employment opportunities and expanding economies. How can we nurture our *ubuntu* in such an environment?

I know of multinational companies that use independent distributors as part of their distribution channels, but they completely stopped selling on credit to many of them because of a lack of trust. The distributors would be offered interest-free credit to double and triple their capital by these companies. Instead of using the interest-free loan to grow their businesses further, some of them would divert the support to other businesses. With such records, these distributors are normally converted to advance payment or cash on delivery which forces them to borrow from banks at high interest rates.

Vishal Mangalwadi, an Indian social reformer, political columnist and renowned author shares his insights on trust and integrity in a YouTube video.[184]

My first experience of a culture of trust was in Holland.

> My host took me to a dairy to buy milk. I had never heard of machines milking cows. No one was selling the milk. My friend just opened the tap and filled his jug. Then he grabbed a bowl filled with cash. He paid in a 20 Guilder note, took the change and started walking away with his milk. I was stunned. I said, 'Man! If you were an Indian, you would take the milk and the money!

It was then that Vishal says he instantly understood why India is so poverty-stricken. He reflected that if the customer took the milk and the money, the dairy owner would have to hire a salesperson, but if the consumer was corrupt why would the supplier be honest? The supplier would add water to increase the quantity of milk. Frustrated by watered-down milk, the consumer would ask the government to appoint an inspector.

> But why should the Inspector be honest? He would take bribes and allow adulterated milk to be sold. The consumer will have to bear the cost of the milk, water, the sales girl, the Inspector, and the bribe – none of which add any value to the milk. In paying for them, the consumer pays simply for his sin. Paying for all this means that you don't have money left to buy products that actually add value, such as milk turned into ice-cream or cheese.

This is what Africa is going through. It is people paying for their sins in so many ways.

Mismanagement, profligacy and the misuse of revenue act as a deterrent to those who may wish to put up a stake in the business. Other ramifications include increasing interest rates from microfinance institutions and commercial banks. The high cost of capital as a result of high interest rates may prompt the business to increase prices, which would slow down sales, which, in turn, may lead to more negative actions.

The same repercussions may arise when employees steal from their company. The cost of doing business increases, financial performance decreases and consequences may include job losses – all because of a lack of integrity.

African enterpreneurs clamour for capital but lenders are unwilling, and those that are willing charge punishing interest rates to include premium for risks of non repayment due to lack of integrity among other factors. Thus paying for own sins, which accelerates the demise of businesses, and further entrench the vicious cycle. It is a poverty within.

A culture of spending not saving

Africa lacks a strong culture of saving. Income is spent, saved or invested, no matter how small the amount. In South Africa, for example, people borrow money in order to buy cell phones. There are whole lines of credit products to facilitate this type of spending. Whether in South Africa or Ghana, Zambia or Tanzania, if money is not invested for any reason, it is very likely to be spent. The saving part of the equation is mostly non-existent.

If we are discouraged from investing because of a lack of trust or confidence, then we find ourselves in another vicious cycle – an extended spending spree. We do not save the little income we earn because it is not an inherent behaviour for us but, at the same time, we do not invest partly because of perceptions of mismanagement and lack of integrity. Thus, we work to spend, an unsustainable equation as economists and finance gurus will confidently tell you.

Some governments in Africa have attempted to come up with loan guarantee programmes and seed capital funding for startups and small businesses through commercial banks. These programmes are meant to cushion the inherent risk faced by commercial banks, which discourages them from financing small businesses. However, these interventions rarely prove successful, partly because of mishandling and high default rates.

On a positive note, Africans and African entrepreneurs, in particular, are very resilient. In the face of headwinds and waves of boom and bust, they continue investing and pushing harder to break through. It is this spirit that keeps Africa going. It keeps the continent afloat. The unfortunate reality is that it does not lift the continent out of poverty. It survives and make some small progress without breaking through the ceiling of prosperity. It is disappointing that many are comfortable with staying afloat, or contented with merely complaining. We need to encourage qualities that would help us progress faster. It has to start from families inculcating right values, our education system to reflect what we want to be and our communities promoting good practices among other ways. We have to change what is in us that does not deliver for us.

Figure 5.1: Vicious cycle of poverty from self-defeating practices, behaviours and cultures

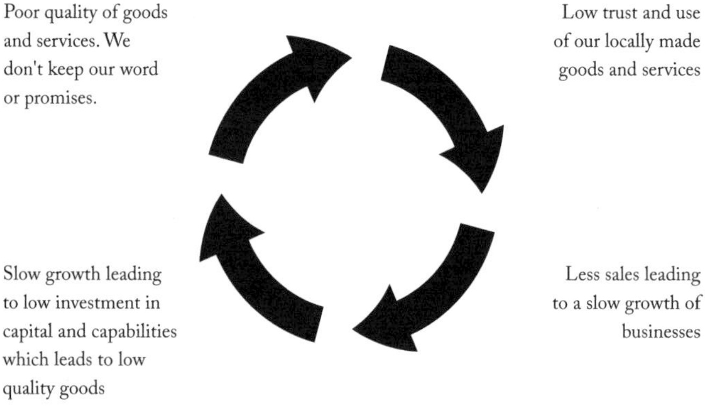

Poor quality of goods and services. We don't keep our word or promises.

Low trust and use of our locally made goods and services

Less sales leading to a slow growth of businesses

Slow growth leading to low investment in capital and capabilities which leads to low quality goods

Source: Author's own

6

Vicious cycle no 6: Business environment and poor regulatory framework

THE MO IBRAHIM Foundation organised an interview in 2019 between Mo Ibrahim, a Sudanese-British billionaire, and the Nigerian Aliko Dangote, Africa's richest man. Both men highlighted a number of issues around doing business across Africa. Below is an abbreviated portion of their interesting conversation.[185]

Mo: In how many countries are you producing cement?

Dangote: Well, 14 in total, the operational ones we have about 11, then we have about three new countries ... In South Africa we have two; in Nigeria we have three, we are building the fourth one ... we have in

Zambia, Tanzania, Ethiopia ... Congo Brazzaville ... in Cameroon ... we are actually building another 3 million tonnes here [Côte d'Ivoire].

Mo: Now, strategically when you begin to build this empire of cement manufacturing, of course you are looking at markets, raw materials and transport but was it necessary to build in 14 countries? Couldn't you build in four or five key locations and then transport to other countries or are there customs barriers forcing you to build factories sometimes where it is not optimum to do so?

Dangote: Well, there are several reasons. One of the reasons, first is that it is not easy to move around. Number two, it depends on the country, whether they have limestone, which is our key raw material.

Mo: That is what I thought…

Dangote: ….let me give you an example because you talked about movement within Africa. Take for instance, our factory in Nigeria, which is in a place called Ibeshe ... We are only 28 kilometres into the Republic of Benin. But the Republic of Benin, they don't allow us to take cement into the Benin Republic but they import from China.

Mo: Why?

Dangote: It is one of the areas that I keep always discussing with my very good friend Vera, I am sure she is seated somewhere here ... (looking around) [referring to Dr Vera Songwe, Executive Secretary of the United Nations Economic Commission for Africa (ECA) And I always tell Vera, please can you make the regional markets in Africa to work before we go to AfCFTA (African Continental Free Trade Area).

Mo: Now, let me just get to the bottom of this. Could it be the Chinese cement is cheaper than your cement?

Dangote: No, no, no, no. If the market is selling for zero, we are willing to compete at zero. So we would just take and sell.

Mo: So how do you compete on price?

Dangote: No, no, no. It's not about competition. It's about allowing us to go in.

Mo: So how come they allow the Chinese and not allow Nigerians?

Dangote: Honestly, Mo, you should ask the president of the country. He will give you better answers.

Mo: Do we have anybody from Benin here? (Silence and some laughs).

Dangote: Because really the AfCFTA is very very good thing … but my issue is even if we sign, what about implementation? You know, we are very good at designing programmes, but implementation is key, which is really missing.

Mo: Because we talked about free trade areas, ECOWAS. We talked about borderless regions. Is that happening in reality or not?

Dangote: Actually, it is not happening in reality ... you know ... because the biggest issue that you would have is allowing movement. Today, if we are going to take cement to say maybe Togo, we are going to spend almost a week for just 210 kilometres.

Mo: Is it the roads or is the Customs?

Dangote: It is the Customs.

Mo: The Customs?

Dangote: Yeah, yeah. You sleep at the border when you get there

Mo: Why?

Dangote: Because, you know ... it is just corruption ...

Mo: You have to pay in order to get your cement across?

Dangote: Well, we don't pay ... maybe that is why they are holding us, but even for the people who are paying, they have to spend that long period of time also. It's a long process. I think the AfCFTA will help us, but I think before we jump into AfCFTA, we must make sure that the regional markets are working very well.

Mo: Right, I think there is some practical issue here, which people need to think about. We keep celebrating in Addis Ababa, signing agreements and free borders and movement, and here we have a situation where it takes a week to move goods 280 kilometres between two neighboring countries.

Dangote: And then your neighbour too will say, 'No, no do not bring your goods here.' You know, I think, when you look at it, a place like Republic of Benin and Togo, they are the ones who will benefit more in terms of these regional markets because, if I am from Benin or if I have business in Benin, it means I don't only have market for 14 or 15 million people, I have Nigeria's market which is 200 million ...

[end of quoted interview]

Many of the African countries do not like to compare their ways of doing things with Western countries. However, it is common knowledge that many countries, especially in Sub-Saharan Africa, do not have strong independent institutions, compared to many developed nations. In some cases, many responsibilities are duplicated among institutions within the public sector.

Onerous bureaucracy exerts pressure on businesses, creating an environment hostile to doing business and impeding commerce from flourishing. Since the continent is developing and is still far behind the curve when it comes to sustainable development, one would expect us to unleash our time and resources to streamline our business environment, helping to fasttrack economic growth and development and enabling us to catch up with the rest of the world. Unfortunately, the very opposite happens.

Quite a number of the policy and regulatory frameworks created choke businesses hence affecting government revenues and constraining economic growth. Inopportunely, the more institutions we create to regulate, the more we complicate processes, which leads to more people looking for ways to avoid the complications and hence low compliance. Low compliance pushes us to create more processes, regulations and more controls. It becomes a vicious cycle of its own and we find ourselves paying for 'sins' of additional costs and slow progress – similar to Vishal Mangalwadi's opposite experience in Netherlands.

Regulations and taxes

As the World Bank points out in its Doing Business 2020 report, 'At its core, regulation is about freedom to do business'.[186] However, in Africa, government agencies and regulations tend to control, choke, block and even punish private enterprises. Even those institutions, which were created for trade facilitation, find themselves falling into the same trap, with burdensome red tape.

The 2014 World Bank report on business[187] showed that in Nigeria there were 47 different taxes that a business needed to pay annually, taking 956 hours to comply. This means it would take approximately 40 days in a year just to comply with paying these taxes. Taking only daylight hours into account, it would take 80 days. Comparatively, the countries of the Organisation for Economic Co-operation and Development (OECD), of which Nigeria is a member, had an average of 12 taxes, which took 175 hours to pay, according to the article done by Deloitte Nigeria.

This was a wake-up call for Nigeria as it was then ranked 170th on the ease of doing business out of 190 countries in 2014, the position it held until almost 2016[188] when the government decided to undertake major reforms to improve its business environment and formed the Presidential Enabling Business Environment Council (PEBEC). Through this council, Nigeria improved drastically, and in less than four years, went up by 39 positions to 131 in 2020.[189] For an African country, this is a significant improvement and reflects what a passion for change and a discontent with the status quo can achieve. One hopes that with this upswing, complacency does not set in.

In 2019, Tanzania abolished 54 different fees and levies, most of which were being charged to farmers.[190] Nonetheless, quite a number of taxes and levies still remained. Tanzania is ranked 141st out of 190 global economies on the ease of doing business index of 2020, which is a three-point improvement from its 144th position rank in 2019.[191]

Whether in Nigeria or Tanzania, it is difficult to conceive how businesses operated in such an environment for such a long time. How would African businesses compete with the rest of the world? Imagine, what progress could have been achieved with a more conducive regulatory environment? Despite the progress being made by some countries, a report on the ease of doing business for 2020 showed that of the lowest ranked ten countries worldwide, seven are African. Considering that compliant businesses were spending 40 days and nights paying their taxes in Nigeria when it ranked 170th, the situation in the bottom seven countries is mindboggling. Only two African countries, Mauritius and Rwanda, featured in the top 50 countries. No wonder the Rwandan economy has been growing at around 8%, on average, for the last 15 years.

It is our mindset – a mindset of holding back and not moving forward. The more institutions we put in place with complicated processes, the more people find ways to avoid the complications, and low compliance is the result. Low compliance pushes us to create more processes and more controls. It becomes a vicious cycle. This is a disease in Africa.

On the tax front, the more complicated the process of complying with regulations and paying tax, the more likely people are to evade taxes. The more people avoid paying taxes, the more government imposes additional and increased taxes, and people find more ways of not paying taxes. With all these cycles we find more taxes strangling businesses, and governments' attempts to expand revenues are increasingly frustrated because of business activity slowing down, which in turn increases non-compliance. The game goes on as spectators on the sidelines watch from outside the continent. We find ourselves paying for our own sins and end up pointing fingers at each other. It is a perfect vicious cycle.

According to the Tax Foundation, an independent tax policy non-profit organisation based in the United States, Africa has the highest average statutory corporate tax rate among all regions in the world, at 28.5%.[192] Comparatively, Europe has the lowest average corporate tax rate among all regions, at 19.99%.

These figures do not take into account other taxes, levies and fees as well as compliance rates. High tax rates do not necessarily lead to higher revenues in the long term, as less disposable income means less spending power for consumers and re-investments for businesses. It is important for Africa to strike a balance between an excessively heavy tax burden that crushes economic activity and drives low compliance versus low taxes that can starve governments and their functioning. With low incomes in Africa and low propensity to save, burdensome taxes only decelerate and pull the continent back in an important marathon.

Unfortunately, the continent is not only faced with issues of multiplicity of taxes and high tax rates; access to capital is also a huge impediment to progress. A World Bank policy research working paper (2020), indicated the highest lending rates in Sub-Saharan Africa region as: Madagascar (60%), Malawi (39%) and Gambia (29%).[193] These are rasping rates for any business while the world average lending rate was 11.57% as of 2019.[194] Whereas there is opportunity to ask the lenders to reduce lending rates, they are also entangled in an environment of their own, with high rate of non-performing loans, high taxes, high inflation in some countries and tough regulatory environments all of which push-up cost of doing business.

Under these environments, our best foot forward leaves the other behind in the mud.

Difficult economic conditions, high lending rates, high tax rates, heavy tax burdens, cumbersome red tape and largely manual processes render the business climate and investment environment unattractive and unpredictable. The continent needs to extricate itself from this harmful cycle, which impacts particularly negatively on start-ups and small and medium-sized businesses, which form the backbone of economies on the continent. We need to 'confess our sins' by repaying our loans, as governments address regulatory environments and lenders retread their operational costs.

Exports

One of the ways to grow our economies in the continent is to boost up exports and intra-continental trading. We must fight to grow our exports. 'Africa accounted for only 2.6% of global trade in 2018, from 2.4% in 2017,' according to Afreximbank's Africa Trade Report 2019.[195]

We need to capitalise on exports to increase our foreign exchange earnings and to tap into opportunities that exist in other markets inside and outside the continent. Export is key for Africa, not only because of the forex earnings, but also because of price realisation. Many markets in Africa command low prices for various reasons, including affordability issues. Improving exports would help to leverage on higher prices available in other markets, which in turn helps on businesses' profitability and better revenue for the governments thereafter. However, there a number of impediments in harnessing these opportunities. Processing of documentation and regulations are among the biggest challenges facing exports from Africa. For instance, it takes 36 days to process export documentations in countries like Angola, Zambia and Niger.[196] When done with documentation and regulatory fights, then logistical and handling inefficiencies will be awaiting.

For example, at one point it was taking four to six weeks in transit to move goods between Ndjamena, the capital city of Chad, to Lagos in Nigeria or Douala in Cameroon at a cost of around US$4500 per 20-foot container, according to one World Bank report.[197] To provide perspective, such a journey usually takes less than a day-and-a-half in a normal private car or SUV. Trucks take a maximum of three to four days. Poor road networks are a contributory factor, as are roadblocks between the two countries, but, more pertinently, it takes around a week for Chadian customs to clear its own goods.

Navigating these weighty regulatory and inefficient systems is not only troublesome for the economy, it adds to the already sizeable costs of doing business in the continent. A 2017 report by the Overseas Development Institute indicated that transport costs in East Africa could fall by 30% if measures were taken to minimize the transit time and costs.[198] This is corroborated with a Japan International Cooperation Agency (JICA) policy paper (2016) indicating that transport of goods in East Africa was 30% higher than in South Asia and up to 60–70% higher than in the United States of America.[199]

A report by Donaldson et al. (2017) under International Growth Centre of London School of Economics and Political Science[200] on 'making transport work for African trade' concluded that the high cost of getting goods to and from borders or ports in Africa were restricting the continent's potential gains from international trade. The report also asserted that the cost of moving goods domestically was higher and could be up to five times that of the United States of America. This is one of a very sad reality that impedes the continent from reaching its full potential. 'Even though the required number of days has been falling, exporters and importers require 50% more time to get exports to market in Africa than in East Asia.'[201]

Africa has regional economic blocs and the AfCFTA for the entire continent. Signatories to this agreement for a tariff-free single African market started in January 1st, 2021. This is the way to go. We need to eliminate in-fighting and unhealthy competition within the blocs and apply growth mindsets that address the question of how we can be successful together. Clean business practices are also very important as are fair and simple regulatory frameworks.

To dissipate the mistrust that cuts across the continent, between individuals, races, communities and countries, enhancing integrity, honesty and trustworthiness is central for our own prosperity. This will increase investment, improve business and, to echo Vishal Mangalwadi, may help to reduce the number of 'sins' for which we need to pay.

Figure 6.1: Vicious cycle of poverty from the business

environment and poor regulatory framework

Source: Author's owm

Less government revenue that forces government to increase taxes and regualtion which leads to unfavourable business environment
Cumbersome regulatory framework and unfriendly business environment
Multiplicity of regulatory institutions, long process and procedures
High cost of doing business leading to poor performance and poor profitability

7

Vicious cycle no 7: Overdependence on nature

AFRICA IS BLESSED WITH an abundance of natural beauty – from forests, rivers and lakes to semi-deserts and deserts, natural valleys like the East Africa's Great Rift Valley, which runs through Uganda, Tanzania, Kenya and Ethiopia, mountains that the eyes of the world regard with awe like Mount Kilimanjaro in Tanzania and Table Mountain in South Africa.

Some of the world's best beaches can be found in Tanzania and on the island of Zanzibar, as well as the Indian Ocean islands of Seychelles and Mauritius on the east coast of Africa. In West Africa, Kokrobite is the most famous seaside resort in Ghana. On the west coast, in the Atlantic Ocean, is the volcanic island of Santo Antao, the second largest island of Cape Verde, with stunning gorges, canyons and valleys.

One cannot talk about Africa's natural wonders without mentioning its national parks. From East Africa's Serengeti National Park in Tanzania and the Masai Mara in Kenya, renowned for their mass migrations of game, and Murchison Falls National Park, Uganda's largest protected area, to the desert wilderness of the Namib-Naukluft Park in Namibia in the south and the wildlife-rich savannah and forests of Mole National Park in Ghana in West Africa, to touch on just a few.

In addition to its natural beauty and pleasant climate, Africa is rich in natural resources. A friend of mine once joked that several African ministers responsible for mineral resources in their countries would not able to list all the types of minerals under their watch because there are so many.

However, such natural blessings have ensnared the continent. The continent sleep dreaming about the natural resources, wake up talking about them and again go to bed thinking about them. We are second to none in bragging about how we are blessed with natural resources. We have become over dependent on nature.

The continent waits to enjoy the fruits of golds, diamonds and copper found in our lands. It waits to benefit from the oil that is drilled, and the new oil fields that are waiting to be drilled. We wait for the rain so that we can carry our hoes and herd our cows. We wait for investors from afar to help us locate and exploit our resources. The continent has long convinced itself that it should wait for foreign tourists to come and appreciate our natural blessings. We cannot be tourists or investors in our own lands. We are waiting! We are waiting for that investor's land or, in South Africa, for the whites' land to be sub-divided among us because their ownership has prevented us from progressing. While much of the rest of the world works their land, devises new inventions and explores new frontiers like the Musk's Mars mission, Africa is awaiting for its nature to respond favorably for it to progress.

TOURISM

Disney theme parks around the world attracted more than 152 million visitors in 2019,[202] which is more than twice the number of tourists who visited the entire continent of Africa that year. The United Nations World Tourism Organisation (UNWTO) reported 80 million international tourist arrivals to Africa in 2019.[203]

Despite all the natural attractions, the entire continent of Africa has only attracted half the number of visitors that flocked to the man-made constructions of Disneyland theme parks. Disney Magic Kingdom theme park in Orlando, Florida lead with 20.96 million visitors in 2019.[204] For the same year, all 54 countries in Africa only attracted 80.2 million visitors.

In contrast, the most visited country in Africa is Morocco, which recorded almost 13 million arrivals in 2019, according to travelandynews.com.[205]

Table 7.1 summarises selected comparative tourist attraction/country visited in 2019.

Table 7.1: Number of tourists in select destinations

Country/Region/Attraction	Tourists in millions in 2019
Africa	80.2
Sub-Sahran Africa	55.3
Morocco	13.1
Kenya	2
Zambia	1.3
Ghana	1
Tanzania	1.5
All Disney	152
Walt Disney World-Orlando	59
Burj Khalifa building-Dubai	6
France	212
Spain	126
United States of America	166

Source: World Bank; Statista; Dubai Tourism Authority

Tanzania, Kenya, Ghana and Zambia, all with stunning natural attractions, had only slightly below 6 million visitors combined while Burj Khalifa, a man-made building in Dubai attracted more than 6 million visitors in 2019.[206] The world is not waiting for nature to deliver for them; they are creating. God created mankind with brains and minds to reform and form, to create and improve. It is great to use nature to enjoy and learn from it, but working to create and form has proved to have far greater value and contribution from iron age, industrial revolution to date.

According to *Business Insider*, in April 2019, Singapore completed an extension of its Changi Airport, with 280 shops and restaurants, an indoor rainforest with more than 900 trees and 60,000 shrubs from around the world making a tiered garden, a waterfall more than 130-feet high at the centre of a four-storey indoor forest, a 164-foot glass pedestrian bridge and walking trails through the butterfly, sunflower, cactus and orchid gardens. The airport is expected to accommodate 50 to 60 million visitors.[207] The Singaporeans are providing new experiences; they are creating things.

Egypt is making some great attempts, too. In early 2021, Egypt announced an ambitious project to build the largest urban park in the continent divided into 20 parks at a cost of US$1.6 billion. The park can accommodate 2 million visitors in a year.[208] Divorcing the continent from depending on nature is a way to go. We need to create knowledge-based economies than be caught in resource- and nature-based economies.

France, Spain and the United States each receive more tourists every year than the entire continent of Africa, despite the continent's unmatched natural escapes and hideaways. France attracts more than twice and a half tourists as much as all 54 African countries combined. France mainly offers great historical sites, museums among other experiences, which is a vast opportunity in such a history-blessed continent. Can the continent keep waiting just to avail itself to what God has blessed it with, without creating add-on experiences? Imagine, for example, a traditional food fair devoted to the continent, possibly offering up to 1,000 different cuisines from our more than 3,000 tribes.

Tourism, a labour-intensive service industry, is one sector that could contribute immensely to turning around the fortunes of our continent.

Where are the vast water activities in our beaches and creative experiences in our forests? Where are the stunning conference facilities and world-class golf courses at close proximity to our national parks where we can attract international meetings? According to the World Economic Forum's Travel and Tourism Competitive index (2019), only three countries in Sub-Saharan Africa – Mauritius, South Africa and Seychelles – score slightly above the globe's travel and tourism competitive average index,[209] while there are many countries that depend on tourism sector in Sub-Saharan Africa.

Contrary to the bragging and reality, the above report indicates that Sub-Saharan Africa performed poorly on travel and tourism competitiveness in the areas of natural and cultural resources. The continent is lagging behind in its own areas of strength and areas it is best known for. The region lags behind in all parameters analysed by the World Economic Forum and we are worse in air transport and airport infrastructure, tourist service infrastructure, cultural resources and business travel as well as natural resources relative to the region's performance in other areas tested.

Tourism accounts for 3.8% of the world's direct employment, while in Africa contributes 2.6% of the total direct employment.[210] On the other hand, Africa only accounts for 5% of the world international arrivals, with Europe scooping half (51%) of the global international visitors.[211] It is great that the African Union's Agenda 2063 highlights tourism as one of the key sectors that can spark rapid growth in the continent. The question remains whether we are investing and innovating enough in this sector to catch up with the rest of the world.

We cannot continue boasting of our natural attractions while garnering only 5% of the world tourists. On a positive note, the continent has enjoyed some good growth on the tourism sector tying up with Asia and the Pacific at 7% ahead of the rest of the world.[212] However, the continent tourists' base is still very low, hence the absolute increment on 7% growth may not be very significant compared to other geographical areas. In the year 2019, Europe grew its international tourists at 5% with a base of 710 million tourists, adding around 36 million tourists in one year compared to around 5 million tourists added in Africa by growing at 7% during the same period.

The more the continent waits for its 'natural blessings' to deliver prosperity, without doing much to signifcantly change course of practise and doing, the more others create and shape their own destinies with their God-given minds and creativity. If we wake up, we will find that we are no different. It is poverty within and not on the skin.

Agriculture

Let us talk about agriculture – our livelihood and the 'father' of all vicious cycles. Almost 70% of the continent's population makes a living through farming.[213] This amounts to around 900 million people, out of Africa's total population of approximately 1.3 billion. This means, it is very difficult to achieve significant transformation in the continent without transforming agriculture in the continent. Ensuring that transformation happens in this sector will trigger the transformation of the entire continent.

According to the Oxford Business Group, the African continent accounts for 60% of the world's arable land, but it only contributes 4% of the world's total agricultural output.[214] In other words, the rest of the world, with 40% of the arable land available to humanity, produces 96% of the world's total agricultural produce. With around 70% of our population engaged in agriculture, yet we only produce 4% of the world's agricultural output despite been blessed with the globe's most arable land, is not only an astonishing fact, but a sobering reality on the continent's face.

Another astounding fact is that with 60% of arable land at hand, Africa is a net food importer. This means, Africa cannot sufficiently supply to meet its own food demand. We have to import from others to survive. As a continent, we lost our status of being a net exporter of agricultural products in the 1980s. We have been experiencing negative growth on net exports of agricultural products, partly because of our high population growth relative to the growth of the agricultural sector.

As we wait for rain and the natural seasons of the year, many countries outside of Africa are creating irrigations systems; creating seeds that increase yield 10- or 20-fold; creating new equipment and machinery to facilitate productivity. We find ourselves still debating whether innovation on seeds is good for us and whether we should fully mechanise our agriculture with such high growing unemployment rates.

Unfortunately, the more we rely on manual labour and unresearched seeds, either by design or by default, the less we produce. No wonder our young people are not interested in agriculture because they have never seen it producing many success stories. All they have seen are their parents toiling on a small farm, day in and day out, from one season to the next. This is what lies in their memories and their minds.

Possibly, this is where the cycle of small thinking starts. For generations, Africans cultivate small farms for household subsistence needs; only managing with a hand hoe or an oxen plough. Why innovate for such a small farm when we can manage with a hand hoe or through oxen ploughing? Additionally, to many, growing crops is not a business, but is meant for the family consumption and only sell a small surplus. These are the mindsets of many Africans who grew up in the villages.

In many parts of Africa, agriculture is not for those who are educated; it is a sector of last resort. It is an ideology that, the educated are supposed to be employed, and those that are neither educated nor interested in business go into agriculture. According to Brookings Institution, Sub-Saharan Africa is home to nearly half of the world's uncultivated land that can be brought into production.[215] This is a huge opportunity for the continent to increase its food production. However, one thing is certain – this cannot be achieved using the hoe or the cow and our reliance on nature like waiting for rains and seasons to make headway in this sector.

This is how vicious cycle kicks in. It is not really feasible to mechanise subsistence farming because of the size of farms. Moreover, the belief that agriculture is not for the elites or the educated is widely held. Those trying to go against these established norms are not welcome. People can come to terms with governments holding huge pieces of land even when they are not farmed or well looked after, but find it unpalatable for private individuals or businesses to own such lands in the name of investors. It is not supposed to be that way. People are supposed to inhabit small farms, not big ones, for the purpose of subsistence farming and to sell the small surplus. There are always villagers who do not have enough land and a portion of someone's larger holdings must be subdivided.

It is a different case for South Africa, where more research and actions need to be carried, but grabbing the land and giving it to black South Africans will not solve the problem. There are several million instances in many other African countries where people have land, which was never taken away from us, but nothing much is happening on these farms, and they are farmed for sustenance.

On the other hand, failures in many parts of Africa should not be an impediment to solving the land issues in South Africa or be used to justify not correcting past mistakes. What if the government buys shares in those farms – say 50% – and sells them as shares instead of actual land, while the farms continue being run by the experienced farmers? It is not the aim of this book to be sucked into the muddy waters of the settler land issue and thus wallow in the luxury of offering simplistic solutions to what is, after all, an extremely complex land issue in South Africa.

A significant segment of African society and its systems do not believe in agriculture for business, even the banks. One would find it very difficult to provide a farm as collateral or security to borrow money from a bank. It is rare to find commercial banks lending to farmers in many parts of Africa. The deep-rooted silent belief that agriculture is not for business has set the stakeholders in the industry into a paradoxical chicken and egg dilemma when it comes to finding a long-term solution. We have even categorised agricultural produce into cash crops and non-cash crops, which are mainly food crops that do not attract export revenue. We can only export cash crops and produce to consume the non-cash crops. Then we wonder why we are not selling as much. These beliefs are well entrenched in our minds and are taught in schools in some countries.

In many parts of Africa, agriculture is for the retired and not for the young and energetic. As for the elites, they only turn to agriculture when they are tired and retired. Even with having 60% of the world's arable land, the number of undernourished is increasing in the continent.[216] These realities and trends must change for the continent to thrive.

Africa's affection for and dependence on nature is not limited to waiting for rain. We use manure from cattle, poultry and so on instead of modern fertilisers because it is in our DNA that natural fertilisers are better. Without dwelling on the debate around whether natural fertilisers are better than artificial ones, the question should be, can Africa mass produce the natural ones? Can it be standardised?

The seeds we use are traditional seeds (natural) and are not well researched. Public agricultural research centres are underfunded. Many small farmers still lack education on seeds and seedlings, and many still use natural traditional seeds believing the seeds produced through seed technology are impregnated with chemicals. Traditional seeds have very low yields. 'Farmers in Africa lose out on tens of millions of euros every year because they use seed that has poor or no germination capacity,' said Marja Thijssen, a researcher from the Wageningen University and Research (WUR) in Netherlands, which was ranked the foremost university for agricultural science in the world in 2020.[217]

The use of pesticides and herbicides is very low in many parts of Africa. Once we plant a seed, we expect it to germinate naturally and produce good yields. Regrettably, nature is neither reliable, nor predictable. Often it turns against us and we do not produce as much. Even when we do produce a surplus, there are no immediate markets. Unfortunately, as we do not have storage facilities, that which cannot be sold immediately ends up rotting. What a piteous vicious cycle.

In the last few years, I visited Germany. While in the country we met with some family friends, a Tanzanian and a Swede that live there. We talked about a potential business, exporting fresh mangoes from Tanzania to Germany, which we had begun discussing a while back. The price of a mango in Germany was 18 times the price of a mango in Tanzania. This presented a lucrative business prospect in our estimation, and some quick maths confirmed it was a viable opportunity.

After a long discussion, we agreed on a list of things to do. For their part, these friends were to share more information on the specific type of mango needed and confirm the value chain on the German side. For my part, I was required to validate the availability of the types of mangoes, the sustainability of supply and the value chain from the Tanzanian side. A few days after our return, I received some voluminous information on the type of mangoes needed, quality and all requirements from the European Union's point of view.

From my side, I had started calling a few acquaintances engaged in farming to solicit information. I was delighted to find out that there was an association of mango growers, which simplified my job. To cut a long story short, I found out that the types of mangoes required were available in Tanzania, but not in the desired quantities. I was also not comfortable with the consistency of supply as there is only one mango season in the country – November through January. It was eye-opening to learn that in many African countries, there is more or less one season of mangoes whereas other countries have more than one season, due to the cultivation of different varieties, with countries like United States having mangoes through the year.[218]

Why do we have only one season when we have one of the

best climates in the world? The answer is clear. The countries with more than one season, and those that have mangoes throughout the year, have invested in researching the different types of mangoes that grow in different climates and seasons. In Africa, most of the mangoes are naturally occurring, do not require special care and produce during their usual season. However, with a single harvesting season and a lack of storage facilities, farmers face the difficult choice of leaving the mangoes to rot or selling them at rock bottom prices.

With all these factors in play, and taking into account the European Union's stringent quality checks, one can conclude as to whether the initially exciting, viable and lucrative business idea was realised.

It is the same problem everywhere. An article in *Reuters* on 25 January 2018 indicated that China sold more than 781,000 tonnes of rice to African countries in 2017, with the Ivory Coast being the largest Chinese rice importer overtaking South Korea.[219]

It is mindboggling to note that the value of global rice imports was US$21.8 billion in 2019, and Africa was the second highest importer, contributing 20.6% of the world's total rice imports, according to worldstopexports.com.[220] This translates to around US$4.5 billion spent on importing rice to Africa. This is equivalent to three-quarter of value of gold exported in 2019 by the second largest exporter of gold in Africa, Ghana,[221] twice as much as the 2019 annual gold exports of Tanzania,[222] which is the sixth largest producer of gold in Africa and is more than three-quarter of Zambia's five-year average export of copper from 2015 to 2020.[223] No African country appears on the list of the top 15 rice exporters, which ship around 92.8% of the world's total rice exports by value.[224]

We need to digest the realities slowly.

According to the Food and Agriculture Organisation of the United Nations (FAO), in 2019 Africa spent a total of US$32.9 billion on the importation of just four products: wheat, maize, palm oil and rice.[225] This is more than the GDP of Togo, Cape Verde, the Central African Republic, Guinea-Bissau, The Gambia, Liberia, Malawi, Lesotho, Eritrea, Comoro and Burundi combined, based on the World Bank's GDP numbers for 2019.[226] Over a period of three years between 2017 and 2019, the continent spent US$101.6 billion in importing the same four products. This is almost equivalent to all 15 West African countries under ECOWAS' 2019 GDP with exception of three countries – Nigeria, Ghana and Cote d'Ivoire. Unfortunately these crops are widely grown across Africa, but we spend a staggering amount of forex to import what the best part of us spend time on.

Perhaps African countries do not talk to each other. North Africa alone imports more than 15 million tonnes of maize valued at US$3.5 billion per year.[227] This is equivalent to the total value of Africa's tea and coffee exports combined. The entire continent exported only US$1.5 billion worth of tea and US$1.8 billion worth of coffee in 2019.[228] The value of exports for these two crops were almost similar in the previous three years from 2018.

The opportunities lie right here in Africa, but we cannot grasp them. As a continent, we import wheat to a total value of US$11.4 billions,[229] which is nearly three times as much as Zimbabwe's total exports as a country in 2018[230] or nearly twice as much as the total of all Cameroon's exports.[231] The biggest importers of wheat on the continent are Egypt, Algeria and Nigeria. Combined, they import around US$6 billions of wheat in 2019.[232] This is just one agricultural product that we import.

As a continent, our top 10 exports of agricultural products

earned us around US$21.4 billion in 2019, while we imported almost twice as much. The value of our top 10 imports of agricultural products was US$42.2 billion in 2019.[233]

Of the top 10 agricultural imports, there is not one crop that is not farmed in Africa. We just cannot meet our own demand even with 60% of the arable land being in our hands. Moreover, even with 'small' that we produce some of our farmers cannot access these markets, while a sizable part of their harvests rots before reaching consumers. It is poverty within.

Adding value to our agricultural products presents a world of immense opportunity for the continent, but we are nowhere close to tapping into it. For instance, the Collaborative Africa Budget Reform Initiative (CABRI), which is an intergovernmental organisation supporting finance ministries within Africa, estimates that cocoa beans have a global value of US$9 billion.[234]

Ivory Coast and Ghana produce and export more than 60% of the world's cocoa beans.[235] The two countries pocket around US$7.5 billion for exporting cocoa beans and related processed cocoa products.[236] However, according to *Business Insider*, the chocolate market was valued at US$103 billion in 2019 in the world.[237] Two countries producing almost two-third of the world's cocoa beans but only making almost less than 10% of the world chocolate market value is clearly leaving too much on the table and an interesting opportunity area for this part of the continent.

The Ivory Coast, which is Africa's leading producer and exporter of cocoa, has, at least, made some headway in adding value to its cocoa crop. The Ivory Coast exports more or less around US$1.2 billion worth of cocoa paste, butter and chocolate a year.[238] This amount is still insignificant compared to the value created globally, but it does signal some progress. If this crop was farmed in one of the European countries or in the USA, it would be fair to say that a significant part of the global value would have remained in their countries. And this is just one crop. We can explore many other crops around the continent and the trend is the same.

India is the largest producer of cotton in the world with an estimated 6.4 million metric tonnes of cotton in 2019/2020[239] but it only exports less than a million tonnes.[240] This means they use over 80% of their production internally, creating additional jobs in the textile industries and adding value to the economy. Cotton cultivation employs around 6 million farmers in India[241] and the textile industry directly employs around 51 million people and indirectly 68 million people.[242]

To make sense of the big impact this one crop has on India's economy, The Jobs For Youth in Africa Strategy 2016–2025, which was crafted by the African Development Bank, targets to create new 25 million jobs for youth.[243] It is understandable that the Indian big employment numbers were created over a long time, but the assertion can only be a proof to us that it is possible and we have to change course with speed.

China is the world's second largest producer of cotton hitting 5.9 metric tonnes of cotton in 2019/2020,[244] but China imported around US$4.4 billion worth of cotton between April 2020 and April 2021,[245] clinching its exports of textiles products at US$150 billion in 2020 despite Covid-19's impact.[246]

Vietnam and Bangladesh are not in the top 10 cotton producers in the world.[247] However, their textile industries, combined, export an approximate total value of US$65 billion – which is around three times the total top 10 agricultural exports for the entire continent of Africa.[248]

To change our course, Africa's agricultural sector needs a total rebuild and revamp rather than a spring-clean. It may prove impossible to change our existing farmers' ways. We may need to create a whole new approach to farming and a fresh set of farmers if we are to forge ahead. It is not only about revamping the land as some of us might think. We will need to completely change our way of thinking, of living and our practices when it comes to this sector.

We might think of the opportunities previously highlighted from a quantitative point of view. However, quality is another part of the equation. Most of the export markets require a very high quality produces. We cannot approach our export markets by cheating the scales as some farmers do in parts of Africa or by cheating on quality by mixing grades of rice, cocoa, coffee or maize.

It was very disappointing to hear, some time back, that some farmers add sand to sacks of their crops to increase the weight, oblivious to the fact that such practices would kill their next opportunity. Many in the continent would be familiar with such behaviour, when we buy simple items such as bananas for our families and the seller would try to palm us off with over-ripe fruit, or when we buy first-grade rice, which is adulterated with rice of inferior quality, or when we are ripped off buying timber that is intentionally not cut to our specifications. Others tamper with the weighing scale just to cheat on the quantity. It is very sad.

These underhand practices have short-term benefits, if at all. Such people cannot appreciate that they will potentially lose a customer and are doing their business a disservice. If we want to prosper and fetch top prices for our products, integrity and honesty is key. There are so many challenges to address, and their resolution must be detailed. We must get our act together if we want to try to exploit the opportunities on and beyond the continent.

We have left too much to nature, while doing little to work with nature to produce more. Israel offers living proof of how to work with and influence nature, using cutting-edge technologies to exponentially increase outputs. Former Israeli Prime Minister Benjamin Netanyahu, speaking in Washington at the American-Israel Public Affairs Committee (AIPAC) on 6 March 2018 said:

> Here's an old industry we were always great at, agriculture. Now we have precision agriculture. See that drone in the sky? Connected to a big database there are sensors in the field, in the field drip irrigation, fertilisation, and now we can target with this tech the water we give, the fertiliser we give, down to the individual plant that needs it. That's precision agriculture, that's Israeli.[249]

This is absolutely stunning. Israel is not waiting for rain and nature to determine their agricultural output; they are shaping their future. We are very far off from these levels of technological advancement, but we cannot give up. We cannot bring up our usual excuses – years after independence, colonialism, the World Bank and IMF, climate change – because others are steering their future. As they appreciate the huge impact of climate change, they are not waiting, they are researching for seeds that are more resistant to certain weather conditions and this is happening at lightning speed. Even those without arable land are ahead of us in agriculture. Nonetheless, taking a positive outlook, the potential is immeasurable.

We have to consciously take some steps to harness the opportunities. We have to start somewhere. Revolutionising African agriculture has become even more critical as the United Nations organisations such as World Food Programme (WFP) and Food and Agriculture (FAO) project that the number of people who face food insecurity would double just in year 2021[250] as a result of Covid-19. This means the impact would have been even bigger given the continuation of Covid-19 in to 2021 and beyond.

The African Development Bank estimates that, by 2030, agri-business in Africa will be worth a potential US$1 trillion.[251] Agriculture is one of the biggest opportunities for the continent, in some ways surpassing minerals and probably oil and gas that have congested our minds for a long time.

Some institutions like the African Development Bank are leading the way to revamp and steer the continent's agriculture sector into the right direction. Initiatives like ENABLE Youth programme, with aim of establishing 10,000 youth-run agribusinesses in every country in Africa,[252] is a sizable and critical action. If such initiatives are engaged with seriously by countries – both public and private sectors – and set concrete, follow-up mechanism to ensure success, then there will be a great step for the continent. Even with significant funding in this sector, other vicious cycles discussed must be taken into consideration and addressed for long term and sustainable progress in the sector. Critical point is we must implement big and move very fast.

Visionary billionaires have already spotted the opportunity and have started making significant investments in agriculture in Africa. This is tremendous progress and possibly heralds a turnaround that will raise the hopes of many and act as an example of Africa's abundant possibilities.

Aliko Dangote is investing about US$2 billion in a rice processing plant in Nigeria. This is captured in his conversation with billionaire Mo Ibrahim during the Mo Ibrahim Foundation forum in 2019.[253]

Mo: ... Tell me, what exactly are you doing in agriculture?

Dangote: Thank you, Mo. Well, what we are doing in agriculture, we are building one million-tonne rice boiling and processing with power generation also attached to them and with this, what we are doing is giving the farmers seeds, apart from seeds with implements, and then, you know, when they finish the harvest we buy, but they have a choice also so that we do not really hold them to ransom, they have a choice of selling to anybody who would offer them a better price.

Mo: So you give them seeds…?

Dangote: We give them seeds, implements and if they need any additional money, we have a backup by our central bank to lend them money as a group to enable them because, you know, in those areas, it is very difficult for them to go and mortgage their houses and borrow money. They can easily borrow money under soft terms. Somebody is not going to ask you to bring your grandmother's certificate of birth, which you normally don't have.

Mo: Okay, but those people when they finish they sell you the rice and you are committed to be competitive…is not because I lend you money, you must give it to me cheap.

Dangote: No, no, no. What we have agreed with them is that if my price is not right, they should give it to somebody but they should come back and pay back the debt…. but you can imagine how many jobs we are going to create.

Mo: How many people are going to work on this?

Dangote: Both that one [rice] and sugar in the next four years we are actually creating about 150,000 jobs.

Mo: 150,000 jobs (applause).

Mo: Interesting, this is one area where Africa...

Dangote: In fact, we are not going to create that much jobs in the refinery which is US$12 billion but this one is just less than US$2 billion, but you can see the amount of jobs. If we really in Africa want to create jobs, prosperity ...

and also somebody was also telling me that there is a great GDP growth here in Cote d'Ivoire but it is not trickling down. Just like us also in Nigeria. When you look at it, even when we are having 7% or 8% of GDP growth, down there, they hardly see anything...

Mo: It is trickling but slowly…

Dangote: It is trickling but slowly, not serious. So, the only way to have this thing trickle down fast enough is through agriculture. And that is where we have greater advantage; you have a ready market, which is the difficulty of a lot of continents, but we have a market because the African continent imports more goods than any other continent. So what we need to do is to make sure we transform our own goods. It is very very important, Mo; let me give you an example. Today between Ghana and Cote d'Ivoire they actually produce two-thirds of the world's cocoa, okay, but the total amount of these exports they have is about US$6 billion, okay, but the chocolate market is US$100 billion. So you can just see that they are just working but working for other people.

Mo: That is very interesting. I hope the points on agriculture register, and that is a very important area because we are not really using all the lands we have. We have huge amounts of arable land that is not been used…

Dangote: 60% of the world's arable land.

Mo: And we are not using that. And even the land we are using has the lowest productivity in the world, and there is a huge upside to improve on productivity, so this is an area people need to look at that very carefully.

Dangote: We have changed that Mo, before you go to the next … you know … on rice… Nigeria we used to do one crop per annum, now we do two crops and they used to get about one to two tonnes per hectare. Now we have varieties that we imported that are giving us up to 8 tonnes per hectare… So once you have this, it will help a lot of people to realise that outlook, farming is not a poor man's business. You can actually get rich faster in farming than doing something else. I mean, you look at it, today we also have fertiliser which we used to import, a lot. This fertiliser, we have laboratories that will go and test your soil and give you what kind of fertiliser that you need, whereas right now, as of today, people use the same fertiliser for maize, for rice, for sugar; so they do not actually differentiate, including the type of soil that you have.

Mo: This is a best practice, why don't you produce a case study or something useful…you have been through that, let other African countries appreciate how to do it because we need to replicate what you have done there and other countries as well, or you want to do it all by yourself (smiles)?

Dangote: (laughs) No, no, no.

Mo: Why do you not really let people know here how to do it and….

Dangote: ...You know Mo, that is one of the reasons when you look at it, I do travel very often to various areas where I give a talk, sometimes inside Nigeria, sometimes outside Nigeria, and just tell them, 'Hey look, all these things are a myth. Nothing is impossible. We can really make it happen. We, as Africans, we can, actually. You know the issue is that first of all we have to understand that in all the countries in the world, whether South Korea, Japan, US; those economies were actually built up by their own indigenous. So if we don't lead in Africa...

Mo: Agriculture was a basis for development of all these countries ... is not backward as people think.

Dangote: It is not backward.

What else can I add to this inspirational conversation? We need to end this vicious cycle of passively depending on nature for our livelihoods. For those who believe in God like I do, I believe that God put man in the Garden of Eden to cultivate and guard it. God created us with brains and minds to form and reform, create and improve. Our destiny as a continent is not tied to nature. Our future is tied to how fast we can divorce ourselves from nature and create our own destiny. We have to rise up and till the land and guard it as the blessing it is.

Figure 7.1: Vicious cycle of poverty from overdependence on nature

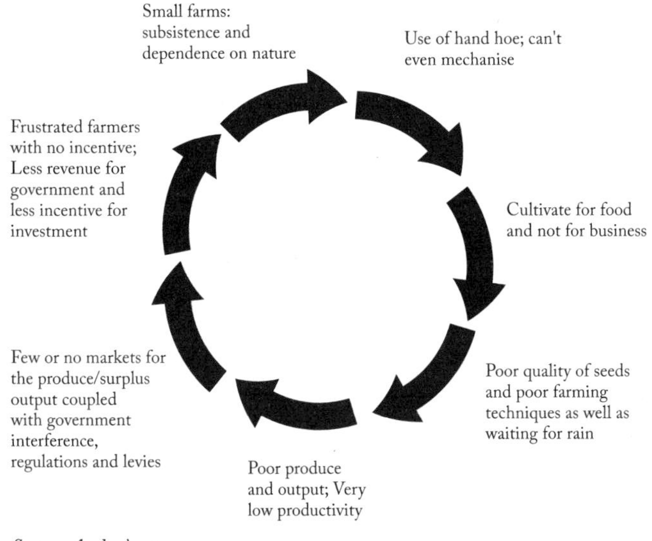

Source: Author's own

8

Vicious cycle no 8: Corruption and political will

One may be tempted to think that if we solved Africa's agricultural issues and emancipated ourselves from our dependence on nature and our tendency to wait for things to happen rather than making them happen, then Africa would blossom, the continent would shine and we could, in a few years, catch up with the rest of the world. However, this outcome is neither inevitable nor easily attainable. There are a few other elephants in the room.

If African continent is to progress, there are dinosaurs to tame – corruption and political will.

Political will

What does 'political will' actually mean?

- The Oxford English Dictionary defines 'political will' as 'the firm intention or commitment of a government to carry through a policy, especially one that is not immediately successful or popular'.
- Democracy Fellow Linn Hammergren, in a 1998 US Agency for International Development (USAID) paper, characterised political will as 'the slipperiest concept in the policy lexicon', calling it 'the *sine qua non* of policy success which is never defined except by its absence'.[254]
- David Roberts of *Vox* took a shot at it and wrote, 'To me, it has always sounded like the political equivalent of the Force in the Star Wars movies. It explains everything and nothing.'[255]

Whatever the term may mean, it misses relevance in Africa in several ways. What is this 'political will' that does not show up, even in discussions against corruption on the continent or about working more closely together as a continent? Talk about reforms in our education systems, and one would say there is no 'political will'. Bring up issues of climate change and the actions that we need to take in addressing its impact elicits the same refrain – the absence of 'political will'.

Talk about land reform or improving revenue collection systems to create efficiencies and fast track service and, suddenly, the lack of 'political will' emerges once more. Air issues of gender imbalance and women empowerment and, I can assure you, the want of 'political will' will show up. Political will would be lacking even in the life and death issues such as hunger.

The United Kingdom-based newspaper *The Guardian* was quoted by *The Week* magazine in 2019 indicating that increase in hunger in some parts of the Africa was largely because of lack of political will: 'but although figures show an improvement in child hunger at a global level, it is getting worse in some parts of Africa, where the problem is largely a question of political will'.[256]

Reports and respected international agencies also emphasise on political will for the continent to transform. Inter Press Service, which is a global news agency, dubbed that Africa needed strong 'political will' to transform agriculture and spur economic growth.[257]

How can we resolve our cross-border business issues without 'political will' coming to the party? How can we fast track customs clearance of trucks at our borders to allow the speedy flow of goods and services and thereby boost our economies? There is no quorum to drive agendas of change when it comes to old and outdated laws, which scar many parts of Africa and hold back the continent's journey to advancement, because 'political will' is missing. Wars and conflicts mar the continent from all angles and corners. Attempts to resolve these life-claiming quagmires has most of the times fallen short as a result of absence of 'political will'. In the world of minerals, this would be a very rare one.

Simply put, maybe 'political will' is the silence of those who matter in making decisions. That is why it is always missing, even when everyone is there.

Corruption

How does 'political will' relate to corruption? The discussions are mainly about corruption as a denial of justice in which individual rights are violated and victims are failed by the judicial system – which is true – but the cost of corruption on the continent is unbearable. It is one of the reasons Africa is marking time and not making progress. Despite commitments and efforts that many African governments have made in fighting against corruption, Transparent International indicates that corruption continues to harm efforts to bring people out of poverty in the continent.[258]

How many times will Africa be willing to re-build its roads, which cost billions of dollars, because of substandard constructions? A standard asphalt road lasts for at least for 15 years and more before major repairs. However, because some roads are built substandard and not because of lack of technical skills, rather as a result of corruption, the continent ends up setting aside budgets to rebuild and reconstruct many roads before their due time, making expansion of road networks in many countries highly constrained.

According to the African Development Bank Group, 'widespread corruption in infrastructure increases project costs, lengthens delivery times, reduces output quality, and thus lowers benefits. It also undermines infrastructure maintenance and sustainability of benefits.'[259]

What about fast-tracking business registrations, easing tax compliance and payments and improving continent's regulatory frameworks? The prevalence of corruption in these areas results in sluggish action, which in turn stalls growth, constrained governments collections and the vicious cycle continues.

The justice system and land tenure system, which are key for the continent's advancement, have been mired in corruption scandals, making reforms in these sectors very difficult.

Africa's hospitals are plagued by corruption scandals, in some cases with people dying because they had nothing in their pockets to extend their lives. If the speed and quality of service is left in the hands of the money hunters seeking bribes, then the continent will never improve its public services and it will take ages to emerge from poverty.

Strangely, part of the Transparency International report,

which was published by the World Economic Forum, shows that the poor pay more bribes than the rich. A survey that was done in 35 African countries revealed that 36% of the poor people paid bribes to access basic public services while 19% of rich people did the same.[260] Could this be the underlining assertion why Africa as a less developed continent is perceived to be more corrupt than the richer countries?

What makes the report extremely sad was an indication that people aged between 18 and 34 were found to be more likely to pay bribes than those over 55 years of age. This is a significant impediment to the progress of the continent not only in the short term but in long run.

Africa is a poor continent that habitually pays high prices for development and infrastructure projects, goods and services, making it even more difficult to make headway in other areas that could have used the premiums paid. An estimate by the African Development Bank in 2018 suggested that the continent's infrastructure needs US$130–170 billion a year, for almost the next decade, with a financing gap in the range of US$68–108 billion to catch up on the infrastructure lag.[261] Currently the continent is spending around 50% to 60% of the above annual estimates. Assuming a 10% corruption factor would mean US$13–17 billion, which is the entire fiscal budget of a medium-to-large African country. Antonio Guterres, the United Nations Secretary General, told Security Council of the United Nations in 2018 that global cost of corruption was at 5% of the global GDP.[262]

Associating the impact of corruption simply with depriving the poorest members of society of justice is a surefire way to ensure corruption remains entrenched. Corruption is in all sectors of the economies and all sections of the community. Corruption is poverty. There is no place on earth that has progressed with prevalent corruption. It affects the entire society. Defeating corruption should probably have been the ninth millennium development goal as it potentially holds back the majority of the existing eight millennium goals.

We have to find the political will to address all these challenges for the much-needed progress of our societies and the continent.

Figure 8.1: Vicious cycle from corruption and political will

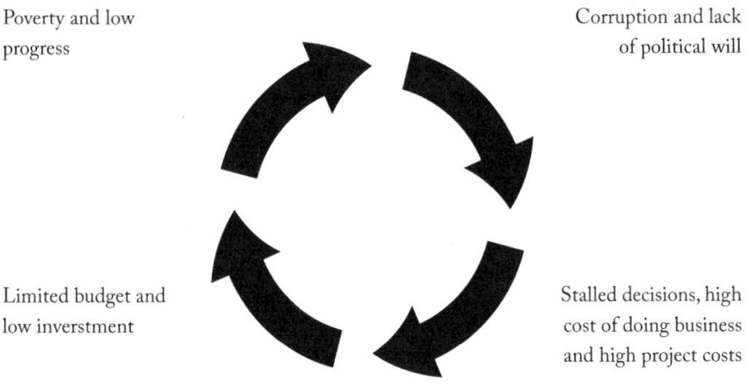

Source: Author's own

9

Vicious cycle no 9: Conflicts and leadership

An Indian general manager with one of the companies in Tanzania visited me for some business. I had known him for a few good years before then, and he had freely spoken with me in many cases. In the midst of our informal business and life discussions, he said, 'Erastus, I will be honest with you. I cannot say this to anyone else, but I am free with you to say it. You Africans have big problems, especially with leadership. Whether it is in business or in other areas of leadership, you have big problems. By the way, you guys cannot handle power, and power goes to your heads very quickly. You forget yourselves, and you have very big egos. Africans cannot handle money or power. What is wrong with you guys?' he asked while twisting his head slantly sideways as many Indians do for emphasis.

Another person of a different nationality who was part of the meeting looked at me with clear uneasiness. He expected me to go through the roof, upset with such remarks, and, probably, lash out with a negative response. But no, as hard as it was to hear, there was an objective small voice telling me that there were some truths in his comments. I told him that it was not correct to generalise that for all Africans, but I agreed with him that a sizable section of us have issues with those elements. We continued with our discussion, and burst out laughing as we made some jokes before he left.

Africa is mired in internal conflicts as it lurches from one fight to another, reaping chaos. We dub this 'Western propaganda', although the reality speaks for itself. Whether this is an exaggerated truth, several parts of the continent are plagued by vicious armed struggles, from tribal or ethnic clashes to politically or religiously motivated conflicts, and have not enjoyed peace for many years. Some countries have never known what the word peace means, and the rest of the continent has almost given up on them, much as the rest of the world has all but given up on us. Conflict and war have become part of life, as in Somalia for example. How many Africans – leaders and citizens – bother when they hear of fights in Somalia or the Democratic Republic of the Congo? It has become a norm.

Hostilities in Somalia, Sudan, the Central African Republic and the Democratic Republic of Congo have been the talk of the continent for many years. I learned about some of these wars in Africa when I was growing up, and now my own children are learning about the same conflicts in school. Thousands of people have died in the bloodshed and the economies of the countries have been held hostage with almost no progress. I started hearing about conflict in the Democratic Republic of Congo – then Zaire – at a young age. Western countries and the country's natural endowments have been blamed. Now, in my adulthood, with my own children going to secondary school, the conflict is still raging and Western countries are still being blamed, only now with the addition of a few fellow African countries in some of the conflicts. We hardly hear anything about the role played by the Congolese leaders and the people, but castigation of the West is everywhere. 'We have nothing to do with it, we comfort ourselves at times.' Don't we really have a role play? The conflict started during the later years of the reign of Mobutu Sese Seko Kuku Ngbendu wa Zabanga, as he used to call himself. We never hear about the failed social and economic structures created by the then Congolese leadership and other actors.

What has happened to us? Even the newest nations, formed in modern times, are steeped in never-ending conflicts.

There was jubilation around the world, and in Africa, celebrating the birth of the 54th nation on the continent after many years of conflict within and without the Republic of Sudan. July 9th 2011 was engraved in their hearts as a 'free at last' day. It was South Sudan's Independence Day. Western and African media were all braced to cover the newest nation born into the world. The *New York Times* proclaimed, 'After years of struggle, South Sudan becomes a new nation' and set the scene in Juba, South Sudan in the first paragraph: 'The celebrations erupted at midnight. Thousands of revelers poured into Juba's steamy streets in the predawn hours on Saturday, hoisting enormous flags, singing, dancing and leaping on the back of cars. 'Freedom!' they screamed.'[263]

The Vice-President of the World Bank's Africa division at the time was Nigerian-born Obiageli Ezekwesili. She recounted her experience of the day in a World Bank blog post titled 'I was there when the Republic of South Sudan was born'.

4:00 AM: I wake up this morning in Nairobi unusually

excited and think to myself, 'Today is actually the Independence Day of South Sudan. Wow. This day has finally come.' I say a word of prayer for the day and get myself ready for the 5:30 a.m. trip to the airport to board our flight to Juba.

> 11:30 AM: We arrive at the venue of the independence celebration to a mammoth crowd excited beyond measure. I find myself thinking of what I missed by being born three years after my own country's independence. Such celebration as a norm only happens once in a lifetime. I have just caught the eyes of a particularly ebullient young woman and I imagine the deep joy of freedom that brings out in her that poignant look of 'All things are possible'. I silently prayed that every one of her good hopes for her country should please come to pass. Such infectious joy ought never to be episodic.[264]

Celebrations were well attended with a record 30 African leaders, then United Nations Secretary General Ban Ki-moon and several senior Western countries' officials, including the former US Secretary of State, Colin Powell. Deutsche Welle (DW) quoted then President of South Africa Jacob Zuma: 'Africans, from the Cape to Cairo, are today walking tall celebrating this historic moment and acknowledging the commitment of the people of both the north and south to peace and progress.'

I celebrated too and it was heartwarming to see a major conflict of the then Sudan ending and birthing of a new nation. As I reflected, I remembered there was more work ahead of them. Out of the contemplation, I gave a young local artist some money to write a song for South Sudan, particularly urging Salva Kiir not to forget why the Sudanese fought for their independence and that peace should reign among them. Unfortunately, the song was never produced.

It took less than two years before all the exuberance and festivities vanished like dust carried away by the wind. Many were heartbroken when in December 2013 the news broke that several people had been killed as conflicts raged between President Salva Kiir and Vice-President Riek Machar. This was a new nation on a new mission, which had fought for so many years for peace, but it couldn't hold it together for two years. As the South Sudanese lifted their feet to take steps to chart their own path to greatness, their hopes unravelled, and they were pushed back into what had consumed their lives for so many years – war. They were back to searching for peace and not for development and this time not with the old enemy but within themselves.

Less than eight years after their independence, Pope Francis couldn't bear the weight of the bloody conflict in South Sudan as he knelt down to kiss President Kiir and Machar's shoes, when they toured the Vatican in April 2019, begging them to reconcile and find peace. 'I'm asking you with my heart,' the Pope said to the president, Salva Kiir, and the opposition leader, Riek Machar, clutching his hands in front of his chest. 'Stay in peace.'[265]

A nation that had thrilled the world, which had cheered it on, was hijacked from within, as the infernal conflict cast them back into a vicious cycle that not only held them back but destroyed whatever small gains had been made. Up until 2020, the conflict had claimed around 400,000 lives and displaced more than 2.24 million people, according to the Council on Foreign Relations, which also tracks global conflicts.[266]

The terrorist attack on the World Trade Center in the USA claimed nearly 3,000 lives and significantly changed the whole world of security and travel. The scrutiny and screening one goes through airports were highly heightened as a result of terrorist act of September 11, 2001 on the twin towers of the World Trade Center. These were necessary and important measures. On the other hand, an African civil war claims 400,000 lives which is more than 130 times the September 11 attack and on top of it the war leaves millions in misery, but life goes on as normal. No one should be tempted to blame the Western countries for not intervening. Africa needs to do more.

The plague of conflict in Africa continues to be a blight inside and outside the continent, as this Wikipedia list as shown in Table 9.1, dating back to 1990, details. Life goes on in most of these areas. Conflict has almost become part of life. While there many other conflicts left out from the list, we have chosen to consider only those started around 1990 onwards or those started earlier but still going on.

Table 9.1: Life-taking conflicts in Africa from 1990 onwards

Country	**Conflicts**
Burundi	• October 21, 1993 – August 2005 Burundi Civil War • September 9, 2002 Itaba Massacre • August 13, 2004 Gatumba Massacre • April 26, 2015 – *ongoing* Burundian unrest
Rwanda	• October 1, 1990 – July 18, 1994 Rwandan Civil War • April 7, 1994 – July 15, 1994 Rwandan genocide
Cameroon	• March 2014 – *ongoing* Boko Haram insurgency • 1 October 2016 – *ongoing* Anglophone Crisis
Central African Republic	• 2004–2007 Central African Republic Bush War • 2012–present Central African Republic Civil War
Kenya	• 2007–2008 Kenyan crisis • 2017 Kenyan general election violence

Country	Conflicts
South Sudan	• May 26, 2009 – *ongoing* Sudanese nomadic conflicts • January 7, 2011 – *ongoing* Ethnic violence in South Sudan • May 19, 2011 – *ongoing* Sudan–SRF conflict • March 26, 2012 – September 26, 2012 Sudan–South Sudan Border War (Heglig Crisis) • December 15, 2013 – February 22, 2020 South Sudanese Civil War
Uganda	• 1987 – *ongoing* Lord's Resistance Army
Chad	• 1998–2002 Civil war in Chad • April 11, 2002– *ongoing* Insurgency in the Maghreb • December 18, 2005 – January 15, 2010 Civil war in Chad
Congo (Republic of)	• Republic of the Congo Civil War (1993–94) • 1997–1999 Republic of the Congo Civil War (1997–1999) • 2016–2017 The Pool War
Congo (Democratic Republic of)	• 1987–*ongoing* Lord's Resistance Army insurgency • 1996–*ongoing* ADF insurgency • October 24, 1996 – May 16, 1997 First Congo War • August 2, 1998 – July 18, 2003 Second Congo War • 1999–*ongoing* Ituri Conflict • 2004–*ongoing* Kivu Conflict • 2012–2013 M23 rebellion • December 2013 – *ongoing* Batwa-Luba clashes • 8 August 2016 – *ongoing* Kamwina Nsapu rebellion
Djibouti	• November 1991 – December 1994 Djiboutian Civil War • June 10, 2008 – June 13, 2008 Djiboutian–Eritrean border conflict

Country	**Conflicts**
Eritrea	• May 6, 1998 – May 25, 2000 Eritrean-Ethiopian War • Eritrean–Ethiopian War (1998–2000) • Eritrean–Ethiopian border conflict (2000–2018) • June 10, 2008 – June 13, 2008 Djiboutian–Eritrean border conflict • Tigray Conflict *spillover in Eritrea; November 3, 2020- ongoing*
Ethiopia	• Ethiopian Civil War *(1974-1991)* • Eritrean–Ethiopian War (1998–2000) • Eritrean–Ethiopian border conflict (2000-2018)–Eritrean border conflict • Tigray Conflict (November 2020- *ongoing*)
Somalia	• January 26, 1991 – *ongoing* Somali Civil War • 1994 – 2019 Insurgency in Ogaden
Comoros	• March 25, 2008 – March 26, 2008 Invasion of Anjouan
Algeria	• 1970 – *ongoing* Western Sahara conflict • December 26, 1991 – February 2002 Algerian Civil War • April 11, 2002 – *ongoing* Insurgency in the Maghreb
Egypt	• January 25, 2011 – *ongoing* 2011 Egyptian Revolution and Aftermath • January 25, 2011 – February 11, 2011 Egyptian Revolution • Egyptian crisis (2011–14) • February 23, 2011 – *ongoing* Sinai insurgency • November 22, 2012 – July 3, 2013 Egyptian protests • June 28, 2013 – July 3, 2013 June 2013 Egyptian protests • July 3, 2013 – *ongoing* Political violence in Egypt • 2013 – *ongoing* Insurgency in Egypt (2013–present)

Country	Conflicts
Libya	• 2011 – *ongoing* Post-civil war violence in Libya • 2014 – *ongoing* Second Libyan Civil War • 1970–*ongoing* Western Sahara conflict • April 11, 2002 – ongoing Insurgency in the Maghreb
Sudan	• April 1983 – January 2005 Second Sudanese Civil War • 1987 – *ongoing* Lord's Resistance Army insurgency • 2003 – *ongoing* War in Darfur • December 18, 2005 – January 15, 2010 Chad-Sudan conflict • May 26, 2009 – *ongoing* Sudanese nomadic conflicts • May 19, 2011 – *ongoing* Sudan–SRF conflict • March 26, 2012 – September 26, 2012 Sudan–South Sudan Border War (Heglig Crisis) • December 19, 2018 - April 11, 2019 (Sudanese 3rd Evolution)
Tunisia	• April 11, 2002 – *ongoing* Insurgency in the Maghreb • December 18, 2010 – January 14, 2011 Tunisian revolution • June 26, 2015 – *ongoing* ISIL insurgency in Tunisia
Angola	• November 11, 1975 to April 4, 2002 Angolan Civil War
Lesotho	• 22 September 1998 – May 1999 South African (SADC) intervention in Lesotho
Mozambique	• May 30, 1977 – October 4, 1992 Mozambican Civil War • 2013–2014 Internal conflict in Mozambique • Jan 2020 – *ongoing* Islamists Rebellion, Cabo Delgado, Mozambique
Namibia	• 1994–1999 Caprivi conflict

Country	Conflicts
Côte d'Ivoire	• September 19, 2002 – March 4, 2007 First Ivorian Civil War • 28 November 2010 – 11 April 2011 Second Ivorian Civil War
Gambia	• 2016–2017 2016–2017 Gambian constitutional crisis • 2017 – ECOWAS intervention in the Gambia (2017)
Guinea-Bissau	• 1997–1999 Guinea-Bissau Civil War
Liberia	• 1989–1996 First Liberian Civil War • 1999–2003 Second Liberian Civil War
Mali	• 1990–1995 Azawad insurgency and Malian civil war • April 11, 2002 – *ongoing* Insurgency in the Maghreb • 2007–2009 Second Tuareg rebellion • 2012 – Third Tuareg Rebellion • 2012 – *ongoing* Northern Mali conflict • August, 2020-Military ousting of President Ibrahim Boubacar
Mauritania	• 1970 – *ongoing* Western Sahara conflict • April 11, 2002 – *ongoing* Insurgency in the Maghreb
Niger	• 1990–1995 First Azawad insurgency • April 11, 2002 – *ongoing* Insurgency in the Maghreb • 2007–2009 Second Azawad insurgency
Nigeria	• 1953 – *ongoing* Religious violence in Nigeria • 1998 – *ongoing* Communal conflicts in Nigeria (1998-present) • 2009 – *ongoing* Niger Delta conflict (2004–present) • 2009 – *ongoing* Boko Haram insurgency
Sierra Leone	• March 23, 1991 – January 18, 2002 Sierra Leone Civil War
Western Sahara	• 1970 – *ongoing* Western Sahara conflict

Source: Wikipedia[267]

Looking at the long list, could one say Africans are probably correct to give up? More than 105 conflicts just from 1990 in 34 countries out of 54 countries. It is a very sad reality. According to Statista, the top 13 African countries had a budget spending on defence of up to US$56.32 billion.[268]

Whatever these figures may mean in terms of value for money, one can make a fair observation to the effect that, in the African context, these weapons are invariably secured for the purpose of fighting enemies who are hardly ever likely to hail from outside the continent. All too often, it is neighbouring countries that are the enemies. Unfortunately, most of the time, it is not even country to country conflicts, most often it is conflicts within countries that have rendered the continent into its knees. How much longer should the continent wait for the Americans and Europeans to resolve these life-embezzling hostilities?

Donald Trump, the former United States president, spoke his mind and heart about African conflicts: 'Africa right now has got problems like few people would even understand,' Trump said in response to a question from Tunisian media. 'They have things going on there that nobody could believe in this room. If you saw some of the things that I see through intelligence, what's going on in Africa, it is so sad. It's so vicious and violent, and we want peace for Africa,' he told told journalists at the NATO summit in Brussels in July 2018.[269]

These 'vicious' and 'violent' confrontations have propelled these countries into a cycle of poverty. Going through the list of these conflicts and the many others that have not been captured here, one must agree that it is indeed 'vicious' and 'violent'. Conflict results in instability. Such countries can't invest in their growing populations, leading to inadequate health and education systems, which result in even less stable societies. High unemployment rates lead to low income, low capital formation, low investment and, in the end, low productivity and production. To complete the cycle, unemployment, illiteracy and poverty spawns more violence, crime and conflict. It is an incessant, vicious cycle of poverty.

It is not the aim of this book to chronicle some political takeover and single out a party to blame – not at all. This work is rather meant to reflect upon how individuals and communities within Africa have been holding back development in the continent and to elucidate what must be addressed to move forward. There is no way Africa can make a meaningful progress as a continent when marred into such deep rampant conflicts.

How can continental leadership embark on a grand campaign for the resolution of these conflicts? Africa strongly supported each other in the fight for independence. Kwame Nkurumah declared Ghana's independence was meaningless unless the whole of Africa was liberated from colonial rule.[270] The same position was taken by Mwalimu Nyerere of Tanganyika then (Tanzania) in supporting Southern African countries to gain their independence.

The African Union is leading the way in trying to resolve these conflicts, but more pressure and actions are needed to bring the scourge to an end. We have to believe that it is possible to have long-lasting peace in Africa and action for it. There are already frameworks to engage and resolve these conflicts but they need to be more effective.

The Peace and Security Council, which came into force in December 2003, is one of the important organs responsible to end conflicts in the continent. Aspiration 4 of the Agenda 2063 aims to achieve 'a peaceful and secure Africa', but the flagship initiative of 'Silencing the Guns by 2020' is lagging behind. The agenda of resolving conflicts in the continent has to be as fiercely urgent as the fight to grow our economies.

There is no time to blame the past. We have to activate already agreed good measures and engage more for political will, get our elders – from retired presidents to respected business and religious leaders – involved in good numbers to bring these sad realities to a closure. It is the 'fierce urgency of now', as in Martin Luther King Jr.'s words. Immediate and long-term adjustments to our education to build strong peaceful societies cannot be over emphasised.

Figure 9.1: Vicious cycle from conflicts and leadership

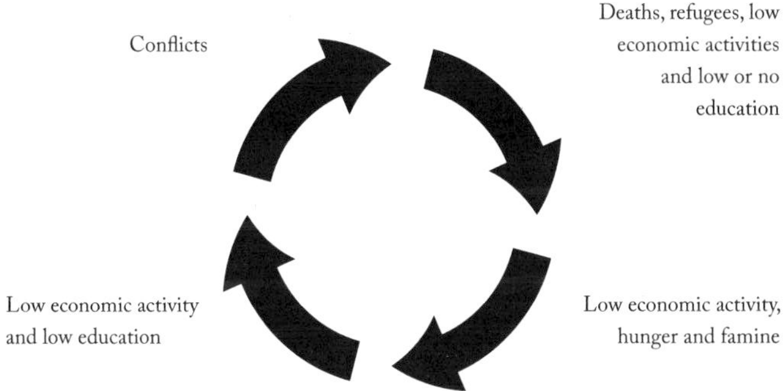

Source: Author's own

10

Vicious cycle no 10: The unfinished business in information and communication technology

How is Africa transforming from an information technology point of view? There are so many loose ends when it comes to information, communication and technology (ICT) in Africa. Indeed, it is an unfinished business. Some would question whether it has started at all, or get excited with sporadic gains made in some parts of the continent. This is an important area that needs systematic address for the continent to sprint to catch up with the rest of the world.

Global technological advancement

The speed at which many parts of the world are changing as

a result of technology and innovation is puzzling. An article published in September 2020 by the World Economic Forum was titled 'The next big disruption is coming. How cities can prepare for 'flying cars'.[271]

A few weeks before the article was published, the Japanese Sky Drive Inc had successfully tested a flying car and was looking forward to commercialising its production. The world of the future is one of driverless or flying cars, and electric cars instead of diesel or petrol cars. From military equipment to agricultural tools and inputs, technological transformation is sweeping and disrupting. The article indicated that some of these technological solutions could be in place within 5 to 10 years. Germany plans to eliminate new diesel or petrol cars by 2030.[272] This is less than 10 years to go. There is a push for the same in large parts of Europe. The United Kingdom had initially planned to ban diesel and petrol cars and vans by 2040. However, they have since revised the timelines, bringing them forward to 2030, which is 10 years earlier than planned.[273] These cars will disrupt the way we think about road construction.

The World Economic Forum article referred above quoted Harrison Wolf, the World Economic Forum's project lead for aerospace and drones, saying 'It is much better to be part of the disruption than to be disrupted – for all stakeholders.' The world's wheel of technological development is turning so fast that many cannot keep up with the pace. The ambition to influence and own the future goes back as far as the dawn of written history. However, the pace of technology-driven change in the last 60 years has been unprecedented. Companies and countries have invested heavily in research and development, leading to accelerated advances in innovations and inventions. A country or company lagging in GDP or revenue growth can now close the gap faster than ever before with the help of technology and innovation. We have witnessed the way South Korea, Singapore and Malaysia transformed over the last six decades on the back of educational transformation and technological investments.

From the below table, DR Congo had higher GDP per capita compared to South Korea in 1960, however, the two countries' GDP per capita are incomparable 60 years down the line, with South Korea having increased its GDP per capita more than 200 times while DR Congo has only double it GDP per capita over the period.

Singapore's GDP per capita was not too far from many African countries either. However, over the 60 years period, Singapore grew its GDP per capita to one of the best in the world while Sub-Saharan countries' GDP per capita remains very low.

Table 10.1: GDP per capita of select countries

Countries	1960	2019
Singapore	US$ 428	US$ 65,233
South Korea	US$ 158	US$ 31,762
Malaysia	US$ 235	US$ 11,415
DR Congo	US$ 220	US$ 581
Zimbabwe	US$ 278	US$ 1,464
Tanzania	US$ 222	US$ 1,122
Ghana	US$ 184	US$ 2,202
Sub-Saharan Africa	US$ 132	US$ 1,596

Source: World Bank Group[274]

The three Asian countries were more or less at the same level of economic prosperity like many African countries. However, from early on they took a different direction, investing in knowledge-based economies, embraced technology and now they are in a different world. Despite the progress made by many

African countries, the two groups are far from each other and almost cannot be compared.

The Asian countries have rapidly invested in manufacturing-related technologies such as robotics, automation, artificial intelligence and 3D printing, thereby reducing the need for and cost of labour inputs. According to the World Economic Forum, South Korea was leading with a number of robots per 10,000 workers in 2016 with 631 robots per 10,000 workers, followed by Singapore, with the German ranking third place while Japan ranked 4th in the world based on number of robots per 10,000 workers as tracked by International Federation of Robotics.[275]

Three years later in 2019, Singapore overtook South Korea leading the world with 918 robots per 10,000 workers which was almost double the number they had in 2016 (488 robots per 10,000 workers). Japan also overtook German to rank third in the world while South Korea ranked second place after Singapore. It is a robot race as the International Federation of Robotics calls it.[276]

It is beyond debate that companies or countries that invest in technology and information technology have the edge, leveraging their advantage to outpace the rest. With almost 0.1% of the world's population, Israel was commanding around 20% of global private investment in cyber security in 2018. It is a whopping investment in one country while the rest of the world shares the remaining 80%. This type of investment could only materialise with a serious investment in education and technology.

Technology and innovation is everything we need to embrace to step change our outlook. A social media company like TikTok, which came into the market in 2017, was valued at US$75 billion in March 2021 and had already topped the list of the most downloaded apps in Playstore. Tesla, an electric car-making campany which released its first car in 2008, is currently the biggest automotive company by market capitalisation (US$582 billion), twice bigger than Toyota Company (US$257 billion) in June 2021.[277] The story of their growth says it all. It is innovation and technology!

As Israeli Prime Minister Benjamin Netanyahu said, speaking at the American-Israel Public Affairs Committee in 2018:

> It's a tremendously strong economy. I'll tell you, we made it stronger by moving Israel to free market principles, which unleashed the spark of genius in our people.
>
> There's a revolution taking place. This couldn't happen at a better time. Look at the top companies in 2006 [projecting a chart of World Largest Companies in 2006 vs 2016] – five energy, one IT. A mere 10 years later – 2016, a blink of an eye in historical terms – it is completely reversed. Five IT companies, one energy company left. The true wealth is in innovation.
>
> You know, these companies – Apple, Google, Microsoft, Amazon, Facebook – guess what? They all have research centres in Israel. Major research centres. And they're not alone, there are hundreds more and there's a reason: something is going on. It's a great change. You want to hear a jargon? This is a terrible sentence, but it's the confluence of big data, connectivity and artificial intelligence. You get that? You know what they do? It revolutionises old industries and creates entirely new industries.[278]

Israel houses most of the research labs belonging to the world's largest companies. This did not happen by chance, but through conscious effort and planning, made possible through strong investment in education and technology.

Israel is largely a desert with little arable land or water. So, they recycle almost 90% of their wastewater. Israel has found solutions to their own problems but is also transforming many parts of the world, as Prime Minister Netanyahu, speaking at the American-Israel Public Affairs Committee in 2018, highlighted this:

> 'I just heard about an African woman in Africa, who has to walk eight hours a day to give water to her children – four hours one way to a well, four hours back. And a young Israeli company brought in this technology that improves on Moses. You remember Moses? He brought water from a rock? They bring water from thin air. They bring water to Africa, to millions of people in Africa – Israeli technology.'

Africa's technological progress

We are not yet in this league and Africa is unprepared for this fast-changing future. Many African countries have good ICT policies, on paper, rather than in practice. Adequate budget and political support is lacking, and human capital is in short supply, as is reliable energy provision, dooming many initiatives to failure. We adopt the new technologies, which will likely leave many still unemployed but, at the same time, we are not creating opportunities to run, maintain or influence these technologies, which would create new sets of job opportunities. Thus, the vicious cycle of poverty grinds on.

For Africa, new technology is a boundless savanna through which to roam; a vast sea in which to swim. However, this sea change is one in which only the prepared will be able to keep their heads above water. Africa is a continent with a sizeable youthful population, which, in the short and medium term, will make up the continent's work force. This presents a huge opportunity for Africa if the natural symbiotic relationship between technology and a young population is effectively exploited. The reverse is true, that if the continent doesn't push hard to explore the opportunities, technology is likely to contribute to Africa being left even further behind. A good example is how Singapore and South Korea changed their economies with the help of technology and innovations and with some African economies trailing 50 to 100 times behind.

We are still fighting to increase our water and electricity accesses. These were some aspects in the first and second revolutions respectively. From the below World Economic Forum summary, one could conclude that the continent is still catching up with the first two revolutions.

Figure 10.1: First to Fouth Industrial Revolution

WORLD ECONOMIC FORUM

Navigating the next industrial revolution

Revolution	Year	Information
1	1784	Steam, water, mechanical production equipment
2	1870	Division of labour, electricity, mass production
3	1969	Electronics, IT, automated production
4	?	Cyber-physical systems

Source: World Economic Forum[279]

Our colonial past may have disqualified us from past 'races', and we can give all the reasons we want for our lacklustre performance – some of which may have some truth – but the fact is that we are not in the running. We need to face this new reality and strategise a way out of it.

With the impact of Covid-19, the transition into the digital space has accelerated, providing more extensive opportunities of greater magnitude. After my discussions with several business leaders across different sectors and industries, it is clear that the digital space will remain an interesting adventure for businesses and consumers, and many young people are grabbing the opportunity with both hands.

Responding to a question asked by one of the employees in a virtual town hall meeting on what he thought might change in businesses post-Covid, the CEO of Coca-Cola Beverages Africa, Jacques Vermeulen, said one of the things that would likely change is the approach to the digital and online interaction space, emphasising that it was time to do things differently. If seasoned big businesses such as Coca-Cola are scratching their heads for different ways of doing business, step changing, and pivoting to lead in the technological space within their own sector, there is no time for smaller businesses, public societies and regulators to relax.

African success stories

Can Africa catch up with the rest of the world at the current pace and extent of its technological transformation? This is a billion dollar question. However, there are some areas of hope and pockets of success within the continent, and some countries have made a good start. The embrace of mobile technology and its penetration in Africa, as well a substantial take up of social media, places the continent on a good footing in its long walk to freedom from poverty.

Africa is advancing very swiftly in mobile phone penetration.

The Global System of Mobile System (GSMA) forecasts that Africa will reach 84% mobile phone penetration by 2025. This is a big step, and we have already witnessed how this type of technology can help change lives on the continent. Mobile money payments and transfers, which started in Kenya with M-PESA, have become not only part of life for many but are transforming ways of doing things on the continent. From paying water and electricity bills, TV subscriptions and taxes, life has been greatly simplified. This is a typical homegrown solution from the continent that is working for the continent. In many ways, it has been a life-changing development. For example, farmers can now receive payment for their produce through mobile money. Otherwise, we would be waiting for Visa or Mastercard or American Express, which would take ages to reach some towns – let alone villages – on the continent.

There are several other success stories emanating from the continent that are changing lives. SafeMotos in Rwanda is Africa's Uber, transforming the way motorcycle transport works. Jumia Food is an online food and drink delivery service similar to Uber Eats, which operates in 11 African countries. Although it closed its Rwandan, Cameroonian and Tanzanian operations in 2019, it is a local solution that has been helping to grow many small to medium food businesses. Local solutions like the Twiga Hosting Limited (THL) in Tanzania provides solutions for accounting software for small businesses at affordable prices as well as providing educational solutions. This beats the big global Enterprise Resource Planning (ERP) software solutions such as Oracle, SAP and even simple systems like QuickBooks by catering for the specific demands of small and medium businesses at affordable prices.

The digital space is changing rapidly and young people are not waiting to take advantage of it. From IT gurus to novices, coding and digitisation are shifting the ways of doing things. The continent's youth are clamouring for local solutions to resolving social and economic problems. In response, CcHub in Nigeria and iHub in Kenya have formed Pan African premier technology innovation centres, which incubate several transformative start-up ventures. Equally, Tanzania Start-Up Association aspires to drive start-up agenda and growth in Tanzania.

Despite the excitement registered across the continent on some progress we are making on ICT and innovation, we are still lagging far behind relative to the rest of the world. According to Brookings Africa Growth Initiative, the continent was lagging behind in 2020 against both developed and developing countries on the Fourth Industrial Revolution when comparing most indicators-infrastructure, technology access and education.[280]

Apart from technological access, we also lagged behind on technology use and technology preparedness relative to other developing countries, developed countries and world average in those indicators. Despite good progress, the continent is making on mobile phone and internet access, we are far behind to allow some sense of satisfaction to settle in. Sometimes we like to throw in the mobile money transfer innovation that originated in Africa that helped to change the continent's money transfers, as a justification to show that we are in the same league.

Sometimes, we look at one hub in one or two cities and feel comfortable being in the race. It's not about a glass half-empty and half-full type of a thing, as some may want to view it. The world is racing with either glass full or glass empty. We cannot use a few good examples to claim being in the same league with Singapore which is leading the world with robots and output they can put on the table.

Education

The world is investing in technology that many of us have never heard of before. Artificial intelligence-assisted healthcare systems, blockchain technology, business intelligence analysis, quantum computing and machine learning, cybersecurity engineering, robotic science and nanotechnology are dramatically changing the world. Technology, science and innovation are very much linked to education. We briefly discussed Africa's education system in a previous chapter. It is sad that our state of education is not the best. We are lagging behind from all fronts and angles, be it from student enrolments to drop outs, teacher-students ratio, lack of essential teaching tools and cramped classes and lecture rooms, just to mention a few.

It is heart-breaking looking at the majority who are left behind after primary education and there is not much option for them. It is a rough road for the continent when it comes to education. All these facts and figures were discussed in the previous chapter and I would consider quality of education as one of the biggest vicious cycles of poverty in the book. How is Africa to compete? Generally, better education systems mean superior information and communication technology sectors. The converse is true for poor education systems.

Our education systems are where the precious minerals of the mind are mined, and success can never be achieved without conscious and proper investment in education. It is through such ventures that nations are changed. Transformation in information technology can never exceed the effectiveness of a country's education system.

In light of the pace of technological changes and the application of artificial intelligence, Jack Ma, founder of Alibaba Group, once said, 'Education is a big challenge now. If we do not change the way we teach, 30 years later, we are in trouble.'[281] He acknowledged that things were changing fast and that the speed of changes might not allow for catching up. We need to be in the 'now' and running fast. That is why many nations are investing in training their populations, especially the youth, and converting sections of their education systems, if not the entire system, to prepare for the 'jobs of the future'. The continent was left behind in all previous three revolutions. Can we catch up with the fourth? Yes, it is possible. However, we have to do more than others to catch up ... run while they are walking... as Julius Nyerere's called.

Jobs of the future/The future of jobs

There has been much debate about whether technological advancement and automation can completely replace human jobs. Something of a consensus has been reached on the likelihood that automation and artificial intelligence will replace many types of jobs but will also create new jobs. That is why there is a talk of 'jobs of the future' – jobs for highly automated, robotic-run, AI-driven businesses or economies. These are jobs that do not currently exist, or do not exist in large numbers, but will be much needed in the future. These are the potential areas where Africa is likely to be left behind if we do not take concrete action – and we cannot be counted with just few representatives. It has to be an aspiration of becoming a big player, influencer and potentially leading in some aspects.

A future of fewer jobs?

While the continent is crying at its mass unemployment, the developed nations are creating equipment and advancing technologies that require fewer human hands. Automation and artificial intelligence is rendering many current manual jobs obsolete. These are huge transformations with serious implications for a continent with more than half of its population still lacking access to electricity.

Many people were amused when *The New York Times* wrote about Amazon having 100,000 robots for handling its warehousing and the impact of this innovation.[282] Later, a video clip went viral on social media showing how these robots were re-arranging shelves and moving books around. It is a reality for advanced economies and may well be a hard certainty for the African continent.

While technological advancement is a huge opportunity, it also threatens to replace swathes of human labour, especially in unprepared nations, as processes are automated and the speed of doing things gathers pace. We haven't really factored in robots. While robots fall into the same category of automation, they are a different story all together. Robotic automation will eliminate repetitive and manual work. Some countries have been experimenting with intelligent robots that can accomplish more complex work. The job replacements for Africa would still be the 'basic' ones, as many of business and government processes are not yet highly automated. However, it is a fast-approaching reality for which we must prepare.

According to the McKinsey Global Institute, robots could replace 800 million jobs by 2030.[283] This is almost three-quarters of Africa's current population. A tweet by the World Bank on 14 August 2020 highlighted this looming reality:

> With robots and automation appearing in more factories, warehouses and stores each year, what does this mean for the future of work?[284]

Robots and automation are not an easy equation for anyone, but it is guaranteed that Africa will be hit hard. African billionaire investor Aliko Dangote confirmed this in his interview with Mo Ibrahim in 2019. The cement production lines in which he is investing in the 2020s differ greatly from those in which he invested previously. The current investments have bigger capacity by far but use fewer people. Talk to any CEO in the manufacturing sector, and he or she will tell you the same. It is the same trend in every industry. Even agriculture – the area upon which most of our population depends – has been revolutionised by technology and does not require as many people as it used to. It is a painful reality with much at stake if Africa does not participate in and strategise with this new future in mind.

This new way of life is inescapable. It may come down to how we choose to view it. If we view it as a threat, then we may try to avoid it, but at our own peril. On the other hand, if we choose to embrace it as an opportunity and put our minds to it, then the conversation changes. We will prepare, and let our young people unleash their unbeatable imaginations, supporting them with the necessary environment and easing capital acquisition for these initiatives. It cannot be by chance; it has to be by design; it has to be a conscious business.

How can we take a seat at the table? These questions are not meant to demoralise us, but encourage us to critically look within, as we cast our eyes to the horizon. The challenges in Africa present opportunities for technological transformation. The continent cannot afford to keep waiting for greater access to water, improved healthcare and better roads.

Despite some encouraging efforts and promising beginnings, we cannot celebrate, fold our hands and take comfort from the fact that we are in the race. We have just begun. We are not yet sufficiently organised so as to be able to accelerate our technological progress and achieve great things. Despite the great work currently being done on the continent in the technology space, we are still scratching the surface given the challenges the continent faces, and the facts and evidence are clear.

We cannot keep waiting for others to solve our problems. We cannot keep relying on charity. Transformation happening in other parts of the world will catch up with us, if we are not prepared. The rest of the world is moving at a supersonic speed and it is not time to think small and move slowly. This is no time to blame others by saying that, 'They automated processes and made machines to cause unemployment in Africa'. We need to participate in defining and building our own future.

We must expand ICT and innovation hubs a hundred fold if this is to be a serious business. We need each university in the continent to have innovation hubs and where applicable ICT hubs. We need to upsurge private sector partnerships x-fold to support these hubs. We cannot measure our achievements by looking at our neighbouring countries; we are almost the same. It requires a completely new horizon. We may need a fresh and different stock market for startup and venture capital hubs to raise funds and capital, without forgetting to address the previous vicious cycles.

We cannot just depend on a belief in ourselves or simply say, 'We will cross that bridge when we come to it.' There is no guarantee that, on the other side of the river, the situation will have improved. While crossing the river, things might have changed and are indeed changing very rapidly. On the other hand, if we only wait on the riverbank, we will not have control over our future and we will have to live with the consequences.

We must have plans and push those plans through to reality. Time is ticking, and the pace of changes is too fast to blink an eye. As the first president of Tanzania, Julius Nyerere, famously said, 'We must run while others walk.' With the advancement of technology we are currently witnessing, one might say, 'We are walking, while others are running.' We too must run, and must start now and must run faster/do more.

We are the sum of our daily conversations, thoughts and actions! We can never be better than our daily conversations, thoughts and actions. We must change the same to reflect the future we want. We cannot change the conversations only, and certainly we cannot change thoughts only to step change things. We must change our conversations, thoughts and actions. It cannot be different! As former President Obama said in a speech to his supporters on 5 February 2008, 'Change will not come if we wait for some other person or some other time. We are the ones we have been waiting for. We are the change that we seek.'[285]

Figure 10.2: Vicious cycle from the unfinished business in

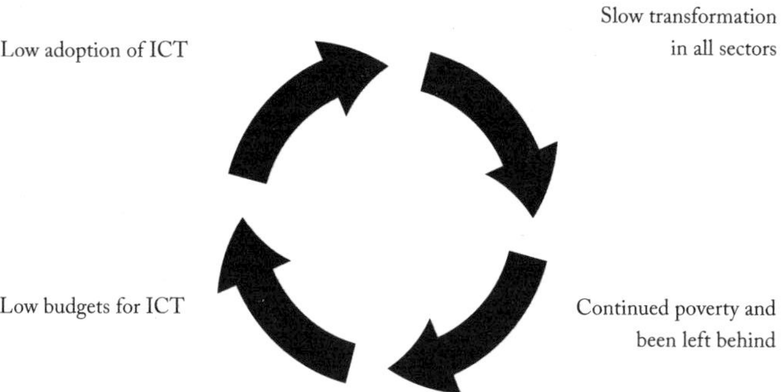

information and communication technology

Source: Author's own

Conclusion

It is a complex situation to be in. There is no silver bullet to any of the challenges the continent faces. It is worse when issues and problems are so entrenched and intertwined causing almost an automatic circular turn that do not guarantee evolution from poverty but rather guarantee it.

Each of the 10 vicious cycles discussed in the previous chapters can almost guarantee poverty on its own. It is worse when a vicious cycle connects to another. When high population growth draws tie-ins with a poor education system and the two join forces with blaming and depending on others, coupled with overdependence on nature, set up on not the best business environment regulatory framework, then it is a special mixed concoction to cement us into poverty. Self-defeating practices, conflicts, corruption and lagging behind on technological advancement act as a seal on the poverty package. It is indeed a poverty within and not the skin.

Africa needs a systematic approach to address these issues. It is not on governments alone as some may be tempted to think. The continent needs to unleash all its societal powers and institutions to address these issues. It is a big challenge to address all of the above at once. It would require focus areas and this book proposes three focus areas:

a) Education: This is a starting point. Africa needs to revamp its entire educational system to one of awareness, knowledge, skills and ultimately competencies. While governments can and should lead us into this journey, it cannot be left to the governments alone. With informed society, population growth issue would be touched. Emphasis on girls education will be part of the solution to high population growth. Enlightened community have fewer conflicts as well. It would require more than a classroom education to change some other mindsets such as settling for less and getting used to problems or eliminating some of the self-defeating practices. It is a journey of awareness, knowledge, skills and competencies.
b) Agricultural transformation: It is scientifically and artistically difficult to attain sustainable transformation in the continent without focusing on transforming a sector that the majority depends on. While others think it may take ages to transform agriculture, it could be to the contrary if significantly rallied. While it may require time to transform from the mindsets of subsistence farming to commercial farming, it may need a set of combined new farmers and new investors to bolster the sector. Governments should take daring steps to dramatically and significantly incentivise agriculture and build an enabling environment around it. It should be a top priority, not for one year but for a long run. We should also approach it boldly and in a big way. It should not be scratch on the surface; it has to be a true revamping of all chains and agents, from seeds, fertilisation, land and regulation policy, markets etc. This

sector has automatic linkage to industries hence the priority should be agriculture, agriculture and agriculture.

c) Technology and innovation: This is another crucial area that the continent cannot leapfrog without. Be it in education or agriculture, we will need technology to transform them. Technology will help us differentiate agricultural transformation discussed above to agricultural revolution of the mid-17th century and late 19th century. It is not only an enabler to transmute all sectors but also a serious danger if we continue lagging behind. It would require significant leadership, institutional and policy change to plan and implement required digital transformation. Many African countries have already embarked on digital transformation, with some embracing electronic government, which is a great start. We need technological and innovation hubs in as many areas as possible. Technology has to be our language and embedded in our actions. It may not necessarily be increasing our ICT budget by 50% or doubling it. It will require doing what is required to transform over a period of set time. It is a survival and transformation.

As continent and society, we have a number of issues to address. However, focusing on the three issues above, in my opinion, will give us a long-range run and sustainability. After all, none of the issues above stand in its own without influence and implication in other sectors and areas. We must come out of these vicious cycles. President Barack Obama put it in a best way 'We did not come to fear the future, we came to shape it'.[286]

Notes

1 United Nations Environment Programme, 'Our work in Africa', United Nations Environment Programme, https://www.unep.org/regions/africa/our-work-africa (accessed 15 July 2020)

2 Melissa Garside, 'Platinum metal reserves worldwide by country 2020', *Statista*, 15 March 2021, https://www.statista.com/statistics/273624/platinum-metal-reserves-by-country/ (accessed 27 March 2021)

3 Moky Makura, 'Making democracy work in Africa', *New African Magazine*, 10 February 2021, http://newafricanmagazine.com/25352/ (accessed 27 February 2021)

4 World Bank 'GDP growth (Annual %) - Sub-Saharan Africa' *Data*, https://data.worldbank.org/indicator/NY.GDP.MKTP.KD.ZG?locations=ZG (accessed 8 August 2020)

5 The United Nations Africa Renewal, 'Africa Rising Forum: Realizing Africa's potential for the future of all its peoples' *Africa Renewal*, https://www.un.org/africarenewal/africa-rising (accessed 30 July 2021)

6 Kate Whitting, '5 facts to know about Africa's powerhouse – Nigeria', *World Economic Forum*, 9 August 2019, https://www.weforum.org/agenda/2019/08/nigeria-africa-economy/ (accessed 5 August 2020)

7 United Nations Educational, Scientific and Cultural Organization, 'Education in Africa', United Nations Educational, Scientific and Cultural Organization, 18 November 2016, http://uis.unesco.org/en/topic/education-africa (accessed 19 September 2020)

8 World Bank, 'Population, Total – Sub-Saharan Africa', *Data*, https://data.worldbank.org/indicator/SP.POP.TOTL?locations=ZG (accessed 8 August 2020)

9 United Nations Educational, Scientific, and Cultural Organization, 'Education in Africa', United Nations Educational, Scientific, and Cultural Organization, 18 November 2016, http://uis.unesco.org/en/topic/education-africa (accessed 29 August 2020)

10 Mamadou Biteye, '70% of Africans make a living through agriculture, and technology could transform their world', World Economic Forum, 6 May 2016, https://www.weforum.org/agenda/2016/05/70-of-africans-make-a-living-through-agriculture-and-technology-could-transform-their-world/ (accessed 28 August 2020)

11 UNICEF, *The State of the World's Children 2019: Children, Food and Nutrition*, UNICEF, New York, 2019

12 United Nations Children's Fund, 'Levels and trends in child malnutrition: Key findings', 2019 edition, https://www.unicef.org/reports/joint-child-malnutrition-estimates-levels-and-trends-child-malnutrition-2019 (accessed 8 August 2020)

13 '58.5 million children in Africa suffering from stunted growth', *Xinhua News Agency*, 10 February 2020, https://newsaf.cgtn.com/news/2020-02-10/58-5-million-children-in-Africa-suffering-from-stunted-growth-NXaBbBY0Ss/index.html (accessed 12 September 2020)

14 Kathleen Beegle and Luc Christiaensen, 'Accelerating poverty reduction in Africa', World Bank, Washington, D.C, 2019. DOI.org (Crossref), doi:10.1596/978-1-4648-1232-3.

15 Niaz M. Asadullah and Savoia Antonio, 'Here's how we can eradicate poverty in Africa faster', *World Economic Forum*, 4 March 2019, https://www.weforum.org/agenda/2019/03/how-africa-can-catch-up-with-the-world-in-the-fight-against-poverty (accessed 26 September 2020)

16 Mukhisa Kituyi, 'The $2.5 trillion African economy: Why a borderless Africa offers best hope for unleashing the continent's potential', *UNCTAD*, 17 December 2019, https://unctad.org/news/25-trillion-african-economy-why-borderless-africa-offers-best-hope-unleashing-continents (accessed 19 September 2020)

17 World Bank 'GDP growth (Annual %) – Sub-Saharan Africa', *Data*, https://data.worldbank.org/indicator/NY.GDP.MKTP.KD.ZG?locations=ZG (accessed 8 August 2020)

18 African Development Bank Group, 'From Debt Resolution to Growth: The Road Ahead for Africa, *African Economic Outlook 2021*, Develhttps://www.afdb.org/en/knowledge/publications/african-economic-outlook (accessed 12 June 2021)

19 African Development Bank Group, 'Developing Africa's Workforce for the Future' *African Economic Outlook 2020* - https://www.afdb.org/en/documents/african-economic-outlook 2020 (accessed 12 June 2021)

20 World Bank, 'GDP growth (Annual %) – China', *Data,* https://data.worldbank.org/indicator/NY.GDP.MKTP.KD.ZG?locations=CN (accessed 1 August 2020)

21 World Bank, 'GDP per capita (Current US$) – Singapore', *Data,* https://data.worldbank.org/indicator/NY.GDP.PCAP.CD?locations=SG (accessed 8 August 2020)

22 World Bank, 'GDP (current US$) – United States', *Data,* https://data.worldbank.org/indicator/NY.GDP.MKTP.CD?locations=US (accessed 29 July 2020)

23 World Bank, 'GDP (Current US$) – Japan', *Data,* https://data.worldbank.org/indicator/NY.GDP.MKTP.CD?locations=JP (accessed 15 August 2020)

24 China State Council, 'China lifts over 68 million people out of poverty in 5 years: Report', *The Economic Times,* 10 February 2018, https://economictimes.indiatimes.com/news/international/business/china-lifts-over-68-million-people-out-of-poverty-in-5-years-report/articleshow/62863326.cms?from=mdr (accessed 22 August 2020)

25 International Monetary Fund, 'Six charts show the challenges faced by Sub-Saharan Africa', IMF African Department, International Monetary Fund, https://www.imf.org/en/News/Articles/2021/04/12/na041521-six-charts-show-the-challenges-faced-by-sub-saharan-africa, (accessed in 8 May 2021)

26 Nicholas Norbrook, 'Tech in Africa: Job killer or job creator?' *The Africa Report.Com,* 24 September 2019, https://www.theafricareport.com/17647/tech-in-africa-job-killer-or-job-creator/ (accessed 29 August 2020)

27 https://eschooltoday.com/learn/the-vicious-cycle-of-poverty/ (accessed 13 February 2020)

28 Maggie Fick, 'Dividend or disaster? Nigeria grapples with demographic conundrum', *Financial Times,* 13 October 2016, https://www.ft.com/content/14962a72-8ebf-11e6-8df8-d3778b55a923 (accessed 12 September 2020)

29 United Nations, Department of Economic and Social Affairs, Population Division, *World Population Prospects 2019: Highlights* (ST/ESA/SER.A/423)

30 'What to do about Africa's dangerous baby boom', *The Economist,* 22 September 2018, https://www.economist.com/leaders/2018/09/22/what-to-do-about-africas-dangerous-baby-boom (accessed 5 September 2020)

31 United Nations Conference on Trade and Development, *Economic Development in Africa Report 2018,* UNCTAD, New York and Geneva, United Nations, 2018.

32 Taoufik Oukessou, Nicolas Vincent, Fatima Hamdaoui, Clémence Vergne, Bertrand Savoye, *Moroccan Companies Development in Africa:*

Reality and Outlook, Ministry of Economy and Finance and The French Development Agency, November 2018, Casablanca, Morocco

33 United Nations, Department of Economic and Social Affairs, Population Division, *World Population Prospects 2017* – Data Booklet (ST/ESA/SER.A/401)

34 Tim Bajarin, 'A distracted, divided U.S. is no match for China's long-term plan for domination?', *Fast Company*, 9 May 2019, https://www.fastcompany.com/90346943/china-long-term-domination-plan-can-beat-a-divided-america. (accessed 12 September 2020)

35 Joe Abah, 'Africa's problem is planning, not implementation!', *Africa Research Institute*, 25 January 2017, https://www.africaresearchinstitute.org/newsite/blog/africas-problem-planning-not-implementation/ (accessed 28 August 2020)

36 World Bank, 'Overview', https://www.worldbank.org/en/country/southafrica/overview (accessed 22 September 2020)

37 Aaron O'Neill, 'South Africa – Unemployment rate 2020', *Statista*, 15 July 2021, https://www.statista.com/statistics/370516/unemployment-rate-in-south-africa/ (accessed 17 July 2021)

38 World Bank, 'Population, Total – Zambia', *Data*, https://data.worldbank.org/indicator/SP.POP.TOTL?locations=ZM (accessed 8 August 2020)

39 United Nations, Department of Economic and Social Affairs, Population Division, *World Population Prospects 2017* – Data Booklet (ST/ESA/SER.A/401)

40 United Nations, Department of Economic and Social Affairs, Population Division, *World Population Prospects 2017* – Data Booklet (ST/ESA/SER.A/401)

41 Andrew Nevin, Omomia Omosomi and Michael Ogunremi, 'Unemployment rate expected to hit 30% amid the effect of COVID19 on the economy', *Nigeria Economic Alert*, September 2020, https://www.pwc.com/ng/en/assets/pdf/economic-alert-september-2020.pdf (30 September 2020)

42 Joe Myers, '19 of the world's 20 youngest countries are in Africa', *World Economic Forum*, 30 August 2019, https://www.weforum.org/agenda/2019/08/youngest-populations-africa/

43 World Bank 'GDP (Annual %) – Nigeria', *Data*, https://data.worldbank.org/indicator/NY.GDP.MKTP.KD.ZG?locations=NG (accessed 16 August 2020)

44 United Nations, Department of Economic and Social Affairs, Population Division, *World Population Prospects 2019*: Highlights (ST/ESA/SER.A/423).

45 Micha Wiebusch and Christina Murray, 'Presidential term limits and the

African Union', *Journal of African Law*, 63, S1, May 2019, pp. 131–60, doi:10.1017/S0021855319000056 (accessed 12 September 2020)

46 'Demographic evolution in Africa: A frenetic population growth', *Atlas Magazine*, 10 October 2019, https://atlas-mag.net/en/article/demographic-evolution-in-africa-population-growth-at-a-frenetic-pace (accessed 2 September 2020)

47 'Demographic evolution in Africa: A frenetic population growth', *Atlas Magazine*, 10 October 2019, https://atlas-mag.net/en/article/demographic-evolution-in-africa-population-growth-at-a-frenetic-pace (accessed 2 September 2020)

48 United Nations, Department of Economic and Social Affairs, Population Division, *World Population Prospects 2019: Highlights* (ST/ESA/SER.A/423).

49 'Africa's first challenge: The youth bulge stuck in 'waithood', Mo Ibrahim Foundation, 10 July 2019. https://mo.ibrahim.foundation/news/2019/africas-first-challenge-youth-bulge-stuck-waithood (accessed 5 September 2020)

50 John Wilmoth, 'How will a population boom change Africa?', *BBC News*, 11 September 2015, https://www.bbc.com/news/world-africa-34188248 (accessed 5 September 2020)

51 African Development Bank, 'Jobs for youth in Africa: Catalyzing youth opportunity Across Africa', AfDB, 2016, https://www.afdb.org/fileadmin/uploads/afdb/Images/high_5s/Job_youth_Africa_Job_youth_Africa.pdf (accessed 5 September 2020)

52 United Nations Educational, Scientific and Cultural Organization, 'Education in Africa', United Nations Educational, Scientific and Cultural Organization, 18 November 2016, http://uis.unesco.org/en/topic/education-africa (accessed 5 September 2020)

53 World Bank, 'Population ages 0-14 (% of total population) - European Union', Data, https://data.worldbank.org/indicator/SP.POP.0014.TO.ZS?locations=EU (accessed 6 September 2020)

54 World Bank, 'GDP growth (Annual %) – Sub-Saharan Africa', *Data*. https://data.worldbank.org/indicator/NY.GDP.MKTP.KD.ZG?locations=ZG (accessed 8 August 2020)

55 World Bank, 'Accelerating poverty reduction in Africa: In five charts', World Bank, 9 October 2019, https://www.worldbank.org/en/region/afr/publication/accelerating-poverty-reduction-in-africa-in-five-charts (accessed 28 August 2020)

56 Bill Gates and Melinda French Gates, 'We are goalkeepers', https://www.gatesfoundation.org/goalkeepers/report/2018-report/ (accessed 2 September 2020)

57 World Bank, 'While poverty in Africa has declined, number of poor has increased', World Bank, March 2016, https://www.worldbank.org/en/region/afr/publication/poverty-rising-africa-poverty-report (accessed 12 September 2020)

58 Justine Parkinson, 'Five numbers that sum up China's one-child policy', BBC News, 29 October 2015, https://www.bbc.com/news/magazine-34666440 (accessed 15 August 2020)

59 World Bank, 'Population, Total – European Union', *Data*, https://data.worldbank.org/indicator/SP.POP.TOTL?locations=EU (accessed 12 August 2020)

60 United Nations, Department of Economic and Social Affairs, Population Division, *World Population Prospects 2019: Highlights* (ST/ESA/SER.A/423)

61 Timo Lange, 'Educating all girls is key for global population size – EU demographic scenarios', EU Science Hub - European Commission, 24 May 2019, https://ec.europa.eu/jrc/en/facts4eufuture/eu-demographic-scenarios/girls-education-global-population-growth (accessed 22 August 2020)

62 'Demographic effects of girls' education in developing countries', Proceedings of a Workshop–in Brief, https://www.nap.edu/read/24895/chapter/1#12 (accessed 8 August 2020)

63 Koutonin Mawuna, 'The myth of overpopulated Africa', Fahamu Network for Social Justice, 19 June 2020, http://www.fahamu.org/ep_articles/mawuna-koutonin-on-the-myth-of-overpopulated-africa/ (accessed 2 September 2020)

64 'Uganda's tourism registers an increase in revenue', Maranatha Tours & Travel, 27 September, 2019, https://www.adventureugandasafaris.com/ugandas-tourism-registers-an-increase-in-revenue/ (accessed 16 September 2020)

65 Max, 'MDG 2: Achieve universal primary education', Millennium Development Goals, 15 May 2017, https://www.mdgmonitor.org/mdg-2-achieve-universal-primary-education/ (accessed 9 September 2020)

66 United Nations Educational, Scientific and Cultural Organization, 'Leading SDG 4 - Education 2030', UNESCO, 9 March 2013, https://en.unesco.org/themes/education2030-sdg4 (accessed 7 August 2020)

67 World Bank, 'Accelerating poverty reduction in Africa: In five charts', World Bank, 9 October 2019, https://www.worldbank.org/en/region/afr/publication/accelerating-poverty-reduction-in-africa-in-five-charts (accessed 28 August 2020)

68 United Nations Children's Fund (UNICEF)/African Union (AU), *Children in Africa: Key statistics on child survival and population*, United Nations Children's Fund, 2019

69 '263 million children and youth are out of school', UNESCO, 18 November 2016, http://uis.unesco.org/en/news/263-million-children-and-youth-are-out-school#:~:text=Over%20a%20fifth%20of%20children,17%20are%20not%20in%20school.&text=In%20every%20region%2C%20older%20youth%20face%20greater%20barriers%20to%20education (accessed 14 August 2020)

70 Adewale Kano Murtala, 'Nigeria has highest number of out-of-school children' *The Guardian Nigeria News - Nigeria and World News*, 25 July 2017, https://guardian.ng/news/nigeria-has-highest-number-of-out-of-school-children/ (accessed 1 August 2020)

71 'The challenge: One in every five of the world's out-of school children is in Nigeria', UNICEF, www.unicef.org/nigeria/education (accessed 20 April 2021).

72 Kevin Watkins, 'Too little access, not enough learning: Africa's twin deficit in education', Brookings, 16 January 2013, https://www.brookings.edu/opinions/too-little-access-not-enough-learning-africas-twin-deficit-in-education/ (accessed 14 August 2020)

73 Sheena Bell et al., 'Opportunities lost: The impact of grade repetition and early school leaving', UNESCO Institute for Statistics, 2012, https://reliefweb.int/sites/reliefweb.int/files/resources/global-education-digest-opportunities-lost-impact-grade-repetition-early-school-leaving-2012-en.pdf (accessed 26 August 2020)

74 Sheena Bell et al., 'Opportunities lost: The impact of grade repetition and early school leaving', UNESCO Institute for Statistics, 2012, https://reliefweb.int/sites/reliefweb.int/files/resources/global-education-digest-opportunities-lost-impact-grade-repetition-early-school-leaving-2012-en.pdf (accessed 26 August 2020)

75 Lukhanyo Mtuta, 'Concern as Western Cape records 39 000 high school drop outs', 28 December 2019, https://www.iol.co.za/weekend-argus/news/concern-as-western-cape-records-39-000-high-school-drop-outs-39780766 (accessed 19 September 2020)

76 United Nations Educational, Scientific and Cultural Organization, 'EFA Global Monitoring Report 2013/4: Teaching and learning: Achieving quality for all Malawi: Fact Sheet', UNESCO, http://www.unesco.org/new/fileadmin/MULTIMEDIA/HQ/ED/GMR/pdf/Malawi_Factsheet.pdf (accessed in 10 September 2020)

77 World Bank, 'School enrolment, tertiary (% Gross) – Sub-Saharan Africa', *Data*, September 2020, https://data.worldbank.org/indicator/SE.TER.ENRR?locations=ZG. (accessed 12 August 2020)

78 Abdi Latif Dahir, 'Africa has too few universities for its fast growing population', *Quartz*, 5 January 2017, https://qz.com/africa/878513/

university-education-is-still-a-dream-many-in-africa-are-yet-to-attain (accessed 8 August 2020)

79 United Nations, Department of Economic and Social Affairs, Population Division, *World Population Prospects: The 2017 Revision, Key Findings and Advance Tables.* Working Paper No. ESA/P/WP/248.

80 'Higher education – Caught in a double bind', *University World News*, 30 March 2018, https://www.universityworldnews.com/post.php?story=20180328162530835 (accessed 23 August 2020)

81 World Bank, 'School enrolment, Tertiary (% Gross) – Sub-Saharan Africa', *Data*, September 2020, https://data.worldbank.org/indicator/SE.TER.ENRR?locations=ZG. (accessed 30 September 2020)

82 World Bank, 'School enrolment, Tertiary (% Gross) – Sub-Saharan Africa', *Data*, September 2020, https://data.worldbank.org/indicator/SE.TER.ENRR?locations=ZG. (accessed 30 September 2020)

83 World Bank, 'School enrolment, Tertiary (% Gross) – Sub-Saharan Africa', *Data*, September 2020, https://data.worldbank.org/indicator/SE.TER.ENRR?locations=ZG. (accessed 30 September 2020)

84 World Bank, 'School enrolment, Tertiary (% Gross) – Ethiopia', *Data*, September 2020, https://data.worldbank.org/indicator/SE.TER.ENRR?locations=ET (accessed 25 September 2020)

85 C. Roby, *5 Ways to Innovate Education in Africa, Inside Development*, Devex, 21 May 2018, https://www.devex.com/news/5-ways-to-innovate-education-in-africa-92772 (accessed 20 December 2020).

86 K. Watkins, 'Too little access, not enough learning: Africa's twin deficit in education' in *This is Africa Special Report: Access + Towards a post MDG development agenda on education*, 2013, https://www.brookings.edu/opinions/too-little-access-not-enough-learning-africas-twin-deficit-in-education/ (accessed 20 December 2020).

87 Valerie Strauss, 'There are 110 kids in each class at a school Melania Trump visited in Malawi', *Washington Post*, 4 October 2018, https://www.washingtonpost.com/education/2018/10/04/there-are-kids-each-class-school-melania-trump-visited-malawi/ (accessed 15 August 2020)

88 Simona Varrella, 'Nigeria: Children per class in elementary schools', *Statista*, https://www.statista.com/statistics/1130142/children-per-class-in-elementary-schools-in-nigeria/ (accessed 8 August 2020)

89 World Bank, 'Pupil-teacher ratio, Primary', *Data*, February 2020 https://data.worldbank.org/indicator/SE.PRM.ENRL.TC.ZS. (accessed 12 August 2020)

90 World Bank, 'Pupil-teacher ratio, Primary', *Data*, February 2020 https://data.worldbank.org/indicator/SE.PRM.ENRL.TC.ZS. (accessed 12 August 2020)

91 Valerie Strauss, 'There are 110 kids in each class at a school Melania Trump visited in Malawi', *Washington Post*, 4 October 2018, https://www.washingtonpost.com/education/2018/10/04/there-are-kids-each-class-school-melania-trump-visited-malawi/ (accessed 15 August 2020)

92 Valerie Strauss, 'There are 110 kids in each class at a school Melania Trump visited in Malawi', *Washington Post*, 4 October 2018, https://www.washingtonpost.com/education/2018/10/04/there-are-kids-each-class-school-melania-trump-visited-malawi/ (accessed 15 August 2020)

93 Cabelihle Mthethwa, 'Grade 4 pupil describes the difficulties of learning under a tree in Cape town' *News24,* 16 April 2021, https://www.news24.com/news24/southafrica/news/grade-4-pupil-describes-the-difficulties-of-learning-under-a-tree-in-cape-town-20210416

94 Keith M Lewin, 'Beyond business as usual: Aid and financing education in Sub-Saharan Africa', *International Journal of Educational Development*, volume 78, October 2020, 102247.

95 Global Partnership for Education, 'A long way to school in Kenya', Blog, Global Partnership for Education, 19 May 2017, https://www.globalpartnership.org/blog/long-way-school-kenya (accessed 26 September 2020)

96 'Rockcilia, secondary scholar, Zambia', Campaign for Female Education, https://camfed.org/why-girls-education/stories/rockcilia/ (accessed 26 September 2020)

97 World Vision, 'School or water: The difficult choice of Ethiopian children', *World Vision*, 2 February 2016, https://www.wvi.org/article/school-or-water-%E2%80%93-difficult-choice-ethiopian-children (accessed 26 September 2020)

98 United Nations Educational, Scientific and Cultural Organization, 'School resources and learning rnvironment in Africa', *Key Results from a Regional Survey on Factors Affecting Quality of Education*, August 2016, http://uis.unesco.org/en/documents (accessed 12 September 2020)

99 United Nations Educational, Scientific and Cultural Organization, 'Literacy rates continue to rise from one generation to the next', Fact Sheet No. 45, September 2017, UNESCO,

100 World Bank, 'Literacy Rate, Adult Total (% of People Ages 15 and above)', *Data*, September 2020, https://data.worldbank.org/indicator/SE.ADT.LITR.ZS?most_recent_value_desc=false (accessed 29 August 2020)

101 Iqbal, Mansoor. 'Africa's Higher Education Landscape.' *QS*, 8 July 2015, https://www.qs.com/africas-higher-education-landscape/ (accessed 5 September 2020)

102 Fredua-Kwarteng, Eric & Kwaku Samuel Ofosu 'How Can Universities Address Spiralling Enrolment?' *University World News*,

16 February 2018, https://www.universityworldnews.com/post.php?story=20180214094656754 (accessed 16 September 2020)

103 Kamau Ngotho, 'Clamour for degrees killed our education system', *The Nation*, 26 December 2017, https://nation.africa/kenya/blogs-opinion/opinion/clamour-for-degrees-killed-our-education-system-1249322 (accessed 12 June 2020)

104 Kamau Ngotho, 'Clamour for degrees killed our education system', *The Nation*, 26 December 2017, https://nation.africa/kenya/blogs-opinion/opinion/clamour-for-degrees-killed-our-education-system-1249322 (accessed 12 June 2020)

105 Goolam Mohamedbhai, 'The revival of polytechnics', *University World News*, https://www.universityworldnews.com/post.php?story=201608230854309 (accessed 15 August 2020)

106 African Union, 'African critical technical skills: Key capacity dimensions needed for the first 10 years of Agenda 2063', African Capacity Building Foundation (ACBF), February 2016, https://opendocs.ids.ac.uk/opendocs/handle/20.500.12413/12847 (accessed 18 September 2020)

107 Goolam Mohamedbhai, 'The importance of polytechnics for Africa's development', *International Higher Education*, 88, Winter 2017

108 Yojana Sharma, 'Major reform as 600 universities become polytechnics', *University World News*, 12 June 2014, https://www.universityworldnews.com/post.php?story=20140612080509913 (accessed 19 September 2020)

109 Yojana Sharma, 'Major reform as 600 universities become polytechnics', *University World News*, 12 June 2014, https://www.universityworldnews.com/post.php?story=20140612080509913 (accessed 19 September 2020)

110 Marguerite Dennis, 'The scramble for Africa's growing student population', *University World News*, 13 February 2020, https://www.universityworldnews.com/post.php?story=20200212123955445 (accessed 5 September 2020)

111 Fiona Harvey, 'Africa's shortage of engineering skills will stunt its growth', *The Guardian*, 14 September 2016, http://www.theguardian.com/global-development/2016/sep/14/africa-shortage-of-engineering-skills-and-female-students-will-stunt-its-growth (accessed 22 September 2020)

112 Admin, 'Employment: The time bomb over Africa', 30 November 2020, https://www.africanewsagency.fr/emploi-et-formation-un-nouveau-paradigme-simpose/?lang=en (accessed 16 January 2021

113 'The struggle to find high quality education in Africa', *University of the People*, 28 November 2017, https://www.uopeople.edu/blog/the-struggle-to-find-high-quality-education-in-africa/. (accessed 29 August 2020)

114 African Union, *The Revised Migration Policy Framework For Africa and Plan of Action (2018–2030)*, AU, Addis Ababa, 2018.

115 International Monetary Fund, *World Economic Outlook: Subdued Demand: Symptoms and Remedies,* Washington, October 2016.

116 'How severe is Africa's brain drain?' Africa at LSE, 18 January 2016, https://blogs.lse.ac.uk/africaatlse/2016/01/18/how-severe-is-africas-brain-drain/ (accessed 1 August 2020)

117 Charlotte McDonald, 'Malawian doctors-are there more in Manchester than Malawi', *BBC News*, 15 January 2012. https://www.bbc.com/news/magazine-16545526 (accessed in 11 July 2020)

118 T.L. Friedman, 'Pass the books, hold the oil', *The New York Times*, 10 March 2012, https://www.nytimes.com/2012/03/11/opinion/sunday/friedman-pass-the-books-hold-the-oil.html (access 24 July 2020)

119 Kamau Ngotho, 'Clamour for degrees killed our education system', *Nation,* 4 July 2020, https://nation.africa/kenya/blogs-opinion/opinion/clamour-for-degrees-killed-our-education-system-1249322 (accessed 15 August 2020)

120 N.N. Mhango, 'Africa's dependency syndrome: Can Africa still turn things around for the better?', 2017, https://www.jstor.org/stable/j.ctvh9vxfj, (accessed 24 December 2020).

121 Amy Kaler and John R. Parkins, 'Food, donors and dependency syndrome(s) in South Sudan', *Sociology of Development*, 1, 3, September 2015, pp. 400–16, doi:10.1525/sod.2015.1.3.400.

122 Jong-Dae Park, 'Assessing the role of foreign aid, donors and recipients: Re-inventing Africa's development', in Jong-Dae Park (ed), *Linking Africa to the Korean Development Model*, Springer International Publishing, 2019, pp. 37–60, doi:10.1007/978-3-030-03946-2_2.

123 Augustine Asante et al., 'Health financing in sub-Saharan Africa: From analytical frameworks to empirical evaluation', *Applied Health Economics and Health Policy*, 18, 6, December 2020, pp. 743–46, doi:10.1007/s40258-020-00618-0 (accessed 16 January 2021)

124 Augustine Asante et al., 'Health financing in sub-Saharan Africa: From analytical frameworks to empirical evaluation', *Applied Health Economics and Health Policy*, 18, 6, December 2020, pp. 743–46, doi:10.1007/s40258-020-00618-0 (accessed 16 January 2021)

125 Augustine Asante et al., 'Health financing in sub-Saharan Africa: From analytical frameworks to empirical evaluation', *Applied Health Economics and Health Policy*, 18, 6, December 2020, pp. 743–46, doi:10.1007/s40258-020-00618-0 (accessed 16 January 2021)

126 Kaci Kennedy McDade Ogbuoji, Kenneth Munge, Gilbert Kokwaro and Osondu, 'Reducing Kenya's health system dependence on donors', Brookings, 2 March 2021, https://www.brookings.edu/blog/future-development/2021/03/02/reducing-kenyas-health-system-dependence-

on-donors/ (accessed 10 April 2021)

127 Osondu Ogbuoji McDade, Ipchita Bharali, Natalie Emery and Kaci Kennedy, 'Closing Africa's health financing gap', Brookings, 1 March 2019, https://www.brookings.edu/blog/future-development/2019/03/01/closing-africas-health-financing-gap/ (accessed 5 September 2020)

128 World Bank, 'GDP per capita (Current US$) – Nigeria', *Data*. https://data.worldbank.org/indicator/NY.GDP.PCAP.CD?locations=NG (accessed 8 August 2020).

129 Paul Adepoju, 'Nigeria faces a health financial cliff edge', *Devex*, 7 January 2019, https://www.devex.com/news/sponsored/nigeria-faces-a-health-financing-cliff-edge-93968 (accessed 15 August 2020)

130 Paul Adepoju, 'Nigeria faces a health financial cliff edge', *Devex*, 7 January 2019, https://www.devex.com/news/sponsored/nigeria-faces-a-health-financing-cliff-edge-93968 (accessed 15 August 2020)

131 Japhet Biegon, '19 years ago today, African countries vowed to spend 15% on health', *African Arguments*, 27 April 2020, https://africanarguments.org/2020/04/19-years-africa-15-health-abuja-declaration/ (accessed 12 August 2020)

132 Organization of Economic Cooperation Development 'Access to water and sanitation in the Sub-Saharan Africa', https://www.oecd.org/water/GIZ_2018_Access_Study_Part%20I_Synthesis_Report.pdf (accessed 15 August 2020)

133 USAID, 'USAID water and development country plan for the Democratic Republic of Congo (DRC)', https://www.globalwaters.org/sites/default/files/DRC%20Country%20Plan%20final.pdf (accessed 8 August 2020)

134 Global Waters, 'Democratic Republic of Congo', https://www.globalwaters.orgcurrent-page (accessed 7 August 2020)

135 Global Waters, 'Democratic Republic of Congo', https://www.globalwaters.orgcurrent-page (accessed 7 August 2020)

136 Lawrence Quartey, 'Ghanaian economist warns against aid dependency', *The Africa Report*, 21 July 2011, https://www.theafricareport.com/8517/ghanaian-economist-warns-against-aid-dependency/ (accessed 26 August 2020)

137 Japhet Biegon, '19 years ago today, African countries vowed to spend 15% on health', *African Arguments*, 27 April 2020, https://africanarguments.org/2020/04/19-years-africa-15-health-abuja-declaration/ (accessed 12 August 2020)

138 Japhet Biegon, '19 years ago today, African countries vowed to spend 15% on health', *African Arguments*, 27 April 2020, https://africanarguments.org/2020/04/19-years-africa-15-health-abuja-declaration/ (accessed 12 August 2020)

139 UNCTAD, *Economic Development in Africa Report 2019*, https://unctad.org/webflyer/economic-development-africa-report-2019 (accessed 15 August 2020)

140 'Just say "no": Dead aid: Why aid is not working and how there is a better way for Africa', *Stanford Social Innovation Review*, Summer 2009, https://ssir.org/books/reviews/entry/dead_aid_dambisa_moyo (accessed 26 September 2020)

141 Matthew Bigg, 'USA: World lines up to help after Katrina - United States of America', *ReliefWeb*, 5 September 2005, https://reliefweb.int/report/united-states-america/usa-world-lines-help-after-katrina (accessed 12 September 2020)

142 Raphie Hayat and Jurriaan Kalf, 'Sub-Saharan Africa: Struggling, but still growing', *Rabo Bank*, 3 December 2015, https://economics.rabobank.com/publications/2015/december/sub-saharan-africa-struggling-but-still-growing/ (accessed 8 August 2020)

143 Raphie Hayat and Jurriaan Kalf, 'Sub-Saharan Africa: Struggling, but still growing', *Rabo Bank*, 3 December 2015, https://economics.rabobank.com/publications/2015/december/sub-saharan-africa-struggling-but-still-growing/ (accessed 8 August 2020)

144 J.D. Park, *Re-Inventing Africa's Development: Linking Africa to Korean Development Model*, Palgrave MacMillan, Pretoria, 2019

145 United Nations, 'Declining aid, rising debt: Thwarting World's Ability to Fund Sustainable Development, Speakers Warn at General Assembly High-Level Dialogue',*Meetings Coverage and Press Releases*, 26 September 2019, https://www.un.org/press/en/2019/ga12191.doc.htm (accessed 12 July 2020)

146 Gbemisola Adeoti, 'African literature and the future', CODESRIA, 2015. Open WorldCat, http://sbiproxy.uqac.ca/login?url=http://international.scholarvox.com/book/88831807 (accessed 8 August 2020)

147 A. Eckert, '"We must run while other walk": African civil servants, state ideologies and bureaucratic practices in Tanzania, from the 1950s to the 1970S', 2014, Open Access chapter, doi: 10.1163/9789004264960_009

148 Michael Jennings, '"A very real war": Popular participation in development in Tanzania during the 1950s & 1960s', *The International Journal of African Historical Studies*, 40, 1, 2007, pp. 71–95.

149 Geir Sundet, 'The Politics of Land in Tanzania' PhD Thesis, 1997, University of Oxford

150 Sean Fleming, 'These are the 5 biggest risks facing sub-Saharan Africa this year', *World Economic Forum*, 3 September 2019, https://www.weforum.org/agenda/2019/09/economic-growth-sub-saharan-africa-challenges-risks/ (accessed 12 June 2020)

151 Max Roser and Esteban Ortiz-Ospina, 'Literacy', *Our World in Data*, August 2016, https://ourworldindata.org/literacy (accessed 11July 2020)

152 Macrotrends, 'Sub-Saharan Africa literacy rate, 1985–2021', https://www.macrotrends.net/countries/SSF/sub-saharan-africa-/literacy-rate'>Sub-Saharan Africa Literacy Rate 1985-2021</a> (accessed 13 May 2021)

153 Max Roser and Esteban Ortiz-Ospina Roser, 'Literacy', *Our World in Data*, August 2016, https://ourworldindata.org/literacy (accessed 11July 2020)

154 Moussa P. Blimpo and Mac Cosgrove-Davies, 'Electricity access in Sub-Saharan Africa: Uptake, reliability, and complementary factors for economic impact', Agence Française de Développement, The World Bank, 2019.

155 Kannan Lakmeeharan, Manji Qaizer, Ronald Nyairo and Harald Poeltner, 'Solving Africa's infrastructure paradox', McKinsey, 6 March 2020, https://www.mckinsey.com/business-functions/operations/our-insights/solving-africas-infrastructure-paradox (accessed 11 July 2020)

156 Kannan Lakmeeharan, Manji Qaizer, Ronald Nyairo and Harald Poeltner, 'Solving Africa's infrastructure paradox', McKinsey, 6 March 2020, https://www.mckinsey.com/business-functions/operations/our-insights/solving-africas-infrastructure-paradox (accessed 11 July 2020)

157 Max Roser and Esteban Ortiz-Ospina Roser, 'Literacy', *Our World in Data*, August 2016, https://ourworldindata.org/literacy (accessed 11July 2020)

158 World Health Organization, 'The Abuja Declaration: Ten Years On', 2010, https://apps.who.int/iris/handle/10665/341162 (accessed 12 September 2020)

159 Ruth Maclean and Simon Marks, '10 African countries have no ventilators: That's Only Part of the Problem' *The New York Times*, 18 April, 2020, https://www.nytimes.com/2020/04/18/world/africa/africa-coronavirus-ventilators.html (accessed 27 September 2020)

160 World Health Organization, 'Fact sheet about malaria', World Health Organization, 1 April 2021, https://www.who.int/news-room/fact-sheets/detail/malaria (accessed 17 April 2021)

161 World Health Organization, 'Fact sheet about malaria', World Health Organization, 1 April 2021, https://www.who.int/news-room/fact-sheets/detail/malaria (accessed 17 April 2021)

162 Abutu Alex, 'Why African governments commit less to R&D funding' *SciDevNet*, 22 December 2017, https://www.scidev.net/sub-saharan-africa/news/african-governments-commit-research-funding/ (accessed 18 July 2020)

163 'Makerere's low-cost ventilator ready to assist Covid-19 patients', *Daily Monitor*, 22 June 2020, https://www.monitor.co.ug/uganda/news/

national/makerere-s-low-cost-ventilator-ready-to-assist-covid-19-patients-1896088 (accessed 18 July 2020)

164 Eurostat Statistics Explained, *Africa-EU International Trade in Goods Statistics*. https://ec.europa.eu/eurostat/statistics-explained/index.php/Africa-EU__international_trade_in_goods_statistics (accessed 29 December 2020)

165 'Africa: GDP, by country 2020', *Statista*, October 2020, https://www.statista.com/statistics/1120999/gdp-of-african-countries-by-country/ (accessed 13 November 2020)

166 'Trade balance of services in Africa 200 –2019,' *Statista*, October 2020, https://www.statista.com/statistics/1180864/trade-balance-of-services-in-africa/ (accessed 13 November 2020)

167 Chiponda Chimbelu, 'Building Africa: Can Europe's construction firms compete with China's?, *DW*, 21 February 2020', https://www.dw.com/en/building-africa-can-europes-construction-firms-compete-with-chinas/a-52435595 (accessed 12 July 2020)

168 The Infrastructure Consortium of Africa, 'Key achievements in the financing of African infrastructure in 2018', https://www.icafrica.org/en/topics-programmes/key-achievements-in-the-financing-of-african-infrastructure-in-2018/ (accessed 12 July 2020)

169 Kannan Lakmeeharan, Manji Qaizer, Ronald Nyairo and Harald Poeltner, 'Solving Africa's infrastructure paradox', McKinsey, 6 March 2020, https://www.mckinsey.com/business-functions/operations/our-insights/solving-africas-infrastructure-paradox (accessed 11 July 2020)

170 Muzi Siyaya, 'Long-term strategy needed to grow black-owned businesses', *Fin24*, 12 November 2017, https://www.news24.com/fin24/Opinion/long-term-strategy-needed-to-grow-black-owned-businesses-20171112 (accessed 9 August 2020)

171 Godwin Maro and Stephen Mnyigumbi, 'A study on contractors' contractual relationship within joint venture projects in Tanzania', *International Journal of Construction Engineering and Management*, 8, 1, 2019, pp. 19–23

172 Morris Kirunga, 'Kenyan savers hit by stumbling Sacco sector', *The Africa Report*, 18 March 2019, https://www.theafricareport.com/10479/kenyan-savers-hit-by-stumbling-sacco-sector/ (accessed 14 August 2020)

173 '312 SACCOS in Uganda suffer fraud, poor governance', *The Independent*, 25 January 2021, https://www.independent.co.ug/312-saccos-in-uganda-suffer-fraud-poor-governance/ (14 August 2020)

174 Galgallo Fayo, 'Why Sh1trn Kenya Saccos are a ticking time bomb?', VIDEO - Business Daily, 11 March 2019, https://www.businessdailyafrica.com/bd/news/why-sh1trn-kenya-saccos-are-a-

ticking-time-bomb-video-2242054 (14 August 2020)

175 Erich Leistner, 'Witchcraft and African development', *African Security Review*, 23, 1, January 2014, pp. 53–77, doi:10.1080/10246029.2013.875048.

176 M. Schwantes, 'Warren Buffet will only hire people with high integrity – here are five ways they separate themselves from the pack', BusinessInsider.com, 17 December 2019, https://www.businessinsider.com/warren-buffett-hire-people-with-integrity-heres-how- to-find-them-9?IR=T#:~:text=Buffett%20said%3A,want%20them%20lazy%20and%20dumb.%22 (accessed 5 July 2020).

177 Michael J. Ritt and Mathew Sartwell, '*Napoleon Hill's Positive Action Plan: 365 Meditations for Making Each Day a Success*', New York, 2007

178 'Zig Ziglar: Full information including bio, books, videos, audios, quotes, seminars, and more', Top Results Academy, http://topresultsacademy.com/authors/zig-ziglar (accessed 19 August 2020)

179 'PEBEC, Lagos Pledge improved business environment for SMEs, others' *The Sun Nigeria*, 17 October 2019, https://www.sunnewsonline.com/pebec-lagos-pledge-improved-business-environment-for-smes-others/ (accessed 29 August 2020)

180 Raphael Obonyo, 'Africa looks to its entrepreneurs', April 2016, https://www.un.org/africarenewal/magazine/april-2016/africa-looks-its-entrepreneurs (accessed 26 September 2020)

181 'Top 10 causes of business failures in Africa', *Think Expand Ltd*, 18 January, 2018, https://www.expandgh.com/top-10-causes-business-failures-in-africa/ (accessed 8 August 2020)

182 'The alarming truth about the number of small businesses in South Africa', *Business Tech*, 25 July 2018, https://businesstech.co.za/news/business/260797/the-alarming-truth-about-the-number-of-small-businesses-in-south-africa/ (accessed 8 August 2020)

183 Martin Hommes and Aksinya Sorokina, 'IFC financing to micro, small, and medium enterprises in sub-Saharan Africa', International Finance Corporation, 2016, https://www.smefinanceforum.org/sites/default/files/2014MSME%2BFactsheet-SSA_0.pdf (accessed 29 September 2020)

184 'Why is the West the least corrupt? - Truth matters' - Vishal Mangalwadi. https://www.youtube.com/watch?v=-sNFukJr7HA (accessed 12 September 2020)

185 Mo Ibrahim Foundation, Mo in conversation with Aliko Dangote, 2019, https://www.youtube.com/watch?v=OBnQ21NSpMw (accessed 29 August 2020)

186 World Bank Group, *Economy Profile of Central African Republic: Doing Business 2020: Comparing Regulations in 190 Economies*, World Bank Group, Geneva, 2020

187 World Bank and World Bank Group, *Doing Business 2015: Going Beyond Efficiency: Comparing Business Regulations for Domestic Firms in 189 Economies*, 12th Edition, World Bank, Geneva, 2014.

188 'Ease of doing business in Nigeria: 2008–2019 Data & 2020–2021 Forecast', https://tradingeconomics.com/nigeria/ease-of-doing-business (accessed 11 Septmber 2020)

189 World Bank Group, *Economy Profile of Central African Republic: Doing Business 2020: Comparing Regulations in 190 Economies*, World Bank Group, 2020

190 Florence Mugarula, '54 trade nuisance fees scrapped', *Daily News*, 14 June 2016, https://dailynews.co.tz/news/2019-06-145d0350e58353d.aspx (accessed 26 September 2020)

191 World Bank Group, *Economy Profile of Central African Republic: Doing Business 2020: Comparing Regulations in 190 Economies*, World Bank Group, 2020

192 Elke Asen, 'Corporate tax rates around the world, 2020', Tax Foundation, 9 December 2020, https://taxfoundation.org/publications/corporate-tax-rates-around-the-world/#Findings (accessed 29 August 2020)

193 Erik Feyen and Igor Zuccardi Huertas, *Bank Lending Rates and Spreads in Emdes : Evolution, Drivers, and Policies*, World Bank, Washington, DC, 2020. DOI.org (Crossref), doi:10.1596/1813-9450-9392

194 'Lending interest rate by country, around the world', TheGlobalEconomy. Com, https://www.theglobaleconomy.com/rankings/lending_interest_rate/ (accessed 8 August 2020)

195 Afreximbank, *African Trade Report 2019*, Afreximbank, 2019.

196 Caroline Freund and Nadia Rocha, 'What constrains Africa's exports?', Working Paper, ERSD-2010-07, World Trade Organization (WTO), Economic Research and Statistics Division, 2010, https://econpapers.repec.org/paper/zbwwtowps/ersd201007.htm (accessed 12 September 2020)

197 World Bank, 'Chad: Trade and Transport Facilitation Audit', https://documents.worldbank.org/en/publication/documents-reports/documentdetail/345051468017457955/Chad-Trade-and-transport-facilitation-audit (accessed 16 July 2020)

198 Linda Calabrese and Andreas Eberhard-Ruiz, 'Trade facilitation, transport costs and the price of trucking services in East Africa', Odi.org, 10 August 2017, https://odi.org/en/publications/trade-facilitation-transport-costs-and-the-price-of-trucking-services-in-east-africa/

199 Japan International Cooperation Agency, Regional Economic Integration in Africa, JICA TICAD VI Policy Papers, Tokyo, 2016

200 Dave Donaldson, Amanda Jinhage and Eric Verhoogen, 'Beyond borders:

Making transport work for African Trade', IGC, 30 March 2017, https://www.theigc.org/publication/beyond-borders-making-transport-work-african-trade/ (accessed 11 September 2020)

201 Dave Donaldson, Amanda Jinhage and Eric Verhoogen, 'Beyond borders: Making transport work for African Trade', IGC, 30 March 2017, https://www.theigc.org/publication/beyond-borders-making-transport-work-african-trade/ (accessed 11 September 2020)

202 'Amusement and theme park attendance worldwide 2019', Statista, https://www.statista.com/statistics/194247/worldwide-attendance-at-theme-and-amusement-parks/

203 World Tourism Organization, *International Tourism Highlights*, 2019 Edition. World Tourism Organization (UNWTO), 2019, DOI.org (Crossref), doi:10.18111/9789284421152.

204 Dewayne Bevil, 'Report: Disney's magic kingdom tops worldwide theme park attendance for 2019', *Orlandosentinel.Com*, 16 July 2020, https://www.orlandosentinel.com/travel/attractions/os-et-disney-theme-parks-attendance-2019-20200716-2ijz56qabfhvxfdctjszmvqv3a-story.html (accessed 4 September 2020)

205 Atraye Guha, 'Morocco's tourism sees record year with 13 million arrivals in 2019 – TAN', *TRAVELANDY NEWS*, 6 February 2020, https://travelandynews.com/moroccos-tourism-sees-record-year-with-13-million-arrivals-in-2019/ (accessed 4 September 2020)

206 'Annual Visitor Report 2019', Dubai Tourism, July 2020, https://www.dubaitourism.gov.ae/en/research-and-insights/annual-visitor-report-2019 (accessed 22 August 2020)

207 Kutya Kupellan, 'Look inside the New R19 billion complex at Singapore's Changi Airport, with a 40-metre indoor waterfall', *Business Insider US*, 29 June 2019, https://www.businessinsider.co.za/look-inside-the-new-13-billion-complex-at-singapores-changi-airport-with-a-130-foot-indoor-waterfall-2019-6 (accessed 12 September 2020)

208 Africa Archives TM's Tweet & quote, 'Egypt is building Africa's largest urban park, The Green River in the New Administrative Capital at a Cost of $1.6 Billion, It Will Cover an Area of 35km. It Will Accommodate over 2 Million Visitors Annually. It Is Divided into 20 Parks with Different Styles and Plants' - Trendsmap. https://www.trendsmap.com/twitter/tweet/1373925943455137794 (accessed 5 September 2020)

209 The World Economic Forum, 'The Travel and Tourism Competitiveness Report 2019, Sub-Saharan Africa', https://reports.weforum.org/travel-and-tourism-competitiveness-report-2019/regional-profiles/sub-saharan-africa (accessed 10 February 2021)

210 Africa Development Bank Group, 'African tourism monitor: The high

5s – Tourism as a pathway to industrialization, integration, quality of life, agriculture, and powering up Africa', https://www.afdb.org/en/documents/africa-tourism-monitor-2018 (accessed 10 February 2021)

211 World Tourism Organization, *International Tourism Highlights*, 2019 Edition. DOI.org (Crossref), doi:10.18111/9789284421152.

212 World Tourism Organization, *International Tourism Highlights*, 2019 Edition. DOI.org (Crossref), doi:10.18111/9789284421152.

213 Adamon N. Mukasa, Andinet D. Woldemichael, Adeleke O. Salami and Anthony M. Simpasa, 'Africa's agricultural transformation: Identifying priority areas and overcoming challenges', African Development Bank, 19 April 2019, https://www.afdb.org/en/topics-and-sectors/initiatives-partnerships/staars-structural-transformation-of-african-agriculture-and-rural-spaces/knowledge-products/full-list-of-staars-publications (accessed 5 September 2020)

214 Marieke Ploegmakers, 'Africa: Untapped potential for agriculture', *All about Feed*, 26 July 2019, https://www.allaboutfeed.net/home/africa-untapped-potential-for-agriculture/ (accessed 26 September 2020)

215 Makhtar Diop, 'Foresight Africa 2016: Banking on agriculture for Africa's future', Brookings, 30 November 2001, https://www.brookings.edu/blog/africa-in-focus/2016/01/22/foresight-africa-2016-banking-on-agriculture-for-africas-future/ (accessed 26 September 2020)

216 Food and Agriculture Organization, 'The number of people suffering from chronic undernourishment in sub-Saharan Africa has increased', FAO, 16 November 2017, http://www.fao.org/news/story/en/item/1062874/icode/ (accessed 26 September 2020)

217 Wageningen University, 'Rankings at Wageningen University & Research,' https://www.wur.nl/en/Education-Programmes/rankings.htm#:~:text=%23115%20in%20the%20world&text=The%20new%20global%20QS%20ranking,125th%20to%20the%20115th%20spot (accessed 26 September 2020)

218 'When are mangos in season? Learn More | National Mango Board', Mango.Org, 1 November 2018, https://www.mango.org/blog-when-are-mangos-in-season/ (accessed 18 September 2020)

219 Josephine Mason and Hallie Gu, 'Grain gain: China's rice exports to Africa surge', *Reuters*, 25 January 2018, https://www.reuters.com/article/china-economy-trade-rice-idINL4N1PJ2ZW (accessed 18 September 2020)

220 Daniel Workman, 'Rice imports by country 2020', https://www.worldstopexports.com/rice-imports-by-country/ (accessed 11 September 2020)

221 'Ghana: Export value of gold, 2015–2019.' *Statista*, June 2020, https://www.statista.com/statistics/1172220/export-value-of-gold-from-ghana/

(accessed 8 August 2020)

222 'Tanzania gold', TanzaniaInvest, 14 June 2021, https://www.tanzaniainvest.com/gold (accessed 15 August 2020)

223 'Zambia exports of copper, 1995–2020', Data, *2021 Forecast*. https://tradingeconomics.com/zambia/exports/copper (accessed 12 September 2020)

224 'Rice exports by country 2020', https://www.worldstopexports.com/rice-exports-country/ (accessed 26 September 2020)

225 Food and Agriculture Organization, 'Commodities by region', FAOSTAT, http://www.fao.org/faostat/en/#rankings/commodities_by_regions_imports (accessed 19 September 2020)

226 World Bank, 'Countries', *Data*, https://data.worldbank.org/country/ (accessed 12 September 2020)

227 Food and Agriculture Organization, 'Commodities by region', FAOSTAT, http://www.fao.org/faostat/en/#rankings/commodities_by_regions_imports (accessed 19 September 2020)

228 Food and Agriculture Organization, 'Commodities by region' *FAOSTAT*, http://www.fao.org/faostat/en/#rankings/commodities_by_regions_imports (accessed 19 September 2020)

229 Food and Agriculture Organization, 'Commodities by region' *FAOSTAT*, http://www.fao.org/faostat/en/#rankings/commodities_by_regions_imports (accessed 19 September 2020)

230 'Zimbabwe trade statistics', World Integrated Trade Solution, https://wits.worldbank.org/CountryProfile/en/ZWE (accessed 12 September 2020)

231 'Cameroon trade statistics', *World Integrated Trade Solution*, https://wits.worldbank.org/CountryProfile/en/CMR (accessed 12 September 2020)

232 Food and Agriculture Organization, 'Countries by commodity', *FAOSTAT*, http://www.fao.org/faostat/en/#rankings/countries_by_commodity_imports (accessed 12 September 2020)

233 Food and Agriculture Organization, 'Commodities by region' *FAOSTAT*, http://www.fao.org/faostat/en/#rankings/commodities_by_regions_imports (accessed 19 September 2020)

234 UNCTAD, 'Economic development in Africa Report 2019 – Rules of Origin for Enhanced Intra-African Trade', UN, 27 August 2019. digitallibrary.un.org, https://digitallibrary.un.org/record/3825235 (accessed 22 August 2020).

235 'Global cocoa bean production in 2018/19 and 2020/21, by country', *Statista*, https://www.statista.com/statistics/263855/cocoa-bean-production-worldwide-by-region/ (re-accessed 10 April 2021)

236 Food and Agriculture Organization, 'Cocoa bean production worldwide by region', *FAOSTAT*, http://www.fao.org/faostat/en/#rankings/

commodities_by_country_exports (accessed 9 September 2020)

237 Abigail Abesamis Demarest, '8 unbelievable facts about the $103 billion chocolate industry', *Insider*, 20 November 2019, https://www.insider.com/chocolate-industry-facts-statistics-consumption-2019-11

238 Food and Agriculture Organization 'Cocoa bean production worldwide by region' *FAOSTAT*, http://www.fao.org/faostat/en/#rankings/commodities_by_country_exports (accessed 9 September 2020)

239 'Leading cotton producing countries worldwide 2019/2020', *Statista*, Setember 2020, https://www.statista.com/statistics/263055/cotton-production-worldwide-by-top-countries/ (accessed 15 August 2020)

240 'Leading cotton exporting countries in 2019/2020 (in 1000 metric tonnes)' *Statista*, https://www.statista.com/statistics/191895/leading-cotton-exporting-countries/ (accessed 30 September 2020)

241 'Cotton farming guide; planting; care; yield; harvesting', *Agri Farming*. https://www.agrifarming.in/cotton-farming-guide (accessed 12 September 2020)

242 'Indian cotton industry: Cotton exporters, manfacturers in India', May 2021, *IBEF*, https://www.ibef.org/exports/cotton-industry-india.aspx (accessed 12 June 2021)

243 African Development Bank, 'Jobs for youth in Africa: Catalyzing youth opportunity across Africa', AfDB, 2016, https://www.afdb.org/fileadmin/uploads/afdb/Images/high_5s/Job_youth_Africa_Job_youth_Africa.pdf (12 September 2020)

244 'Leading cotton producing countries worldwide 2019/2020', *Statista*, September 2020, https://www.statista.com/statistics/263055/cotton-production-worldwide-by-top-countries/ (accessed 15 August 2020)

245 'China: Monthly cotton imports 2021', *Statista*, May 2021, https://www.statista.com/statistics/275891/chinas-monthly-cotton-imports/ (accessed 12 June 2021)

246 'China's textile exports topped $150 billion in 2020, up 30%', CGTN, 27 March 2021, https://news.cgtn.com/news/2021-03-27/China-s-textile-exports-topped-150-billion-in-2020-up-30--YY2nwLLSJa/index.html (accessed 10 February 2020)

247 'Top cotton producing countries in the world', *WorldAtlas*, 7 September, 2020, https://www.worldatlas.com/articles/top-cotton-producing-countries-in-the-world.html (accessed 25 September 2020)

248 Food and Agriculture Organization, 'Commodities by regions – Exports', *FAOSTAT*, http://www.fao.org/faostat/en/#rankings/commodities_by_regions_exports (accessed 12 September 2020)

249 'Benjamin Netanyahu addresses 2018 AIPAC Confab', Haaretz.Com, https://www.haaretz.com/israel-news/full-text-benjamin-netanyahu-

addresses-2018-aipac-confab-1.5883524 (accessed 19 September 2020)

250 World Bank, 'Remarks by World Bank Group President David Malpass to the World Food Programme Executive Board', 16 November 2020, https://www.worldbank.org/en/news/speech/2020/11/16/remarks-by-world-bank-group-president-david-malpass-to-the-world-food-programme-executive-board (accesssed 12 January 2021)

251 African Development Bank, 'Africa Agribusiness, a US$1 Trillion Business by 2030', African Development Bank - Building Today, a Better Africa Tomorrow, 8 Feb. 2019, https://www.afdb.org/en/news-and-events/africa-agribusiness-a-us-1-trillion-business-by-2030-18678 (accessed 19 September 2020)

252 African Development Bank, 'The Time for Africa is Now – We can't Slow Down, we Must Quicken the Pace – Adesina Akinwumi', 5 February, 2019, https://www.afdb.org/fr/news-and-events/the-time-for-africa-is-now-we-cant-slow-down-we-must-quicken-the-pace-adesina-17011 (accessed 15 August 2020)

253 Mo in Conversation with Aliko Dangote. www.youtube.com, https://www.youtube.com/watch?v=obnq21nspmw (accessed 29 August 2020)

254 L. Hammergren, *Political Will, Constituency Building, and Public Support in Rule of Law Programs*. Center for Democracy and Governance Bureau for Global Programs, Field Support, and Research U.S. Agency for International Development, Washington DC, 1998, https://issat.dcaf.ch/download/2200/19056/Hammergren%2520Political%2520Will.pdf (accessed 22 August 2020)

255 David Roberts, 'What is "political will" anyway? Scholars take a whack at defining it', *Vox*, 17 February 2016, https://www.vox.com/2016/2/17/11030876/political-will-definition (accessed 22 August 2020)

256 'Child hunger in Africa due to lack of political will', *The Week UK*, 6 June 2019, https://www.theweek.co.uk/101593/child-hunger-in-africa-due-to-lack-of-political-will (accessed 22 August 2020)

257 Busani Bafana, 'Africa needs strong political will to transform agriculture and spur economic growth', Inter Press Service, 17 September 2018, http://www.ipsnews.net/2018/09/africa-needs-strong-political-will-transform-agriculture-spur-economic-growth/ (accessed 9 September 2020)

258 Transparency International, 'Where are Africa's billions?', Transparency.Org, 11 July 2019, https://www.transparency.org/en/news/where-are-africas-billions (29 August 2020)

259 African Development Bank, *African Economic Outlook 2018*, https://www.icafrica.org/fileadmin/documents/Knowledge/GENERAL_INFRA/

AfricanEconomicOutlook2018.pdf (accessed 12 September 2020)

260 Kate Whitning,'1 in 4 Africans had to pay a bribe to access public services last year', *World Economic Forum*, 29 June 2019, https://www.weforum.org/agenda/2019/07/africa-corruption-bribe-economy/ (accessed 12 September 2020)

261 Olivia Ndong Obiang and Solange Kamuanga, '2018 African Economic Outlook: African Development Bank makes a compelling case for Africa's Industrialization', African Development Bank – Building Today, a Better Africa Tomorrow, 31 January 2019, https://www.afdb.org/en/news-and-events/2018-african-economic-outlook-african-development-bank-makes-a-compelling-case-for-africas-industrialization-17776 (accessed 22 August 2020)

262 United Nations, 'Global cost of corruption at least 5 per cent of world gross domestic product, Secretary-General tells Security Council, citing World Economic Forum data', Meetings Coverage and Press Releases, 10 September 2018, https://www.un.org/press/en/2018/sc13493.doc.htm (accessed 1 August 2020

263 Jeffrey Gettleman, 'After years of struggle, South Sudan becomes a new nation', *The New York Times*, 9 July 2011. https://www.nytimes.com/2011/07/10/world/africa/10sudan.html (accessed 5 September 2020)

264 Gregg Benzow and Timothy Jones,, 'World congratulates South Sudan on independence', *DW*, 9 July 2011, https://www.dw.com/en/world-congratulates-south-sudan-on-independence/a-15222851 (accessed 19 September 2020)

265 Jason Horowitz, 'Pope Francis, in plea for South Sudan peace, stuns leaders by kissing their shoes', *The New York Times,* 11 April, 2019, https://www.nytimes.com/2019/04/11/world/europe/pope-francis-south-sudan.html (accessed 15 August 2020)

266 'Civil war in South Sudan', Global Conflict Tracker, https://cfr.org/global-conflict-tracker/conflict/civil-war-south-sudan (accessed 22 August 2020)

267 https://en.wikipedia.org/wiki/List_of_conflicts_in_Africa

268 'Leading African countries for defense spending budget as of 2021 (in million US Dollars', *Statista*, 2021, https://www.statista.com/statistics/1219612/defense-spending-budget-in-africa-by-country/ (accessed 10 July 2021)

269 'Trump: Africa is vicious and violent, immigration is taking over Europe', *Africa Times*, 12 July 2018, https://africatimes.com/2018/07/12/trump-africa-is-vicious-and-violent-immigration-is-taking-over-europe/ (accessed 12 September 2020); United States Embassy in Estonia, 'Remarks by President Trump at Press Conference After NATO summit',

NATO Headquarters, Brussels, 12 July 2018 https://ee.usembassy.gov/remarks-by-president-nato-summit/(accessed 12 September 2020)

270 'Julius Nyerere: "Without Unity, There Is No Future for Africa"', *New African Magazine*, 26 July 2012, https://newafricanmagazine.com/3234/ (accessed 14 August 2020)

271 Linda Lacina, 'The next big disruption is coming. How cities can prepare for flying cars", weforum.org, 15 September 2020, https://www.weforum.org/agenda/2020/09/flying-cars-are-the-next-big-disruption-how-cities-can-prepare/ (accessed 14 August 2020)

272 'Germany plans to ban combustion engine cars by 2030', *Autocar*, 16 June 2016, https://www.autocar.co.uk/car-news/industry/germany-plans-ban-combustion-engine-cars-2030 (accessed 14 August 2020)

273 Roger Harrabin, 'Ban on new petrol and diesel cars in UK from 2030 under PM's Green Plan', *BBC News*, 18 November 2020, https://www.bbc.com/news/science-environment-54981425 (accessed 2 January 2021)

274 World Bank, 'GDP per capita (Current US$) – Ghana' | Data. https://data.worldbank.org/indicator/NY.GDP.PCAP.CD?locations=GH (accessed 1 August 2020)

275 Rob Smith, 'South Korea has the greatest density of robot workers', World Economic Forum, 18 April 2018, https://www.weforum.org/agenda/2018/04/countries-with-most-robot-workers-per-human/ (accessed 8 August 2020)

276 IFR, 'Robot race: The world´s top 10 automated countries', IFR International Federation of Robotics, https://ifr.org/ifr-press-releases/news/robot-race-the-worlds-top-10-automated-countries (accessed 15 August 2020)

277 'Largest automakers by market capitalization', https://companiesmarketcap.com/automakers/largest-automakers-by-market-cap/ (accessed 16 August 2020)

278 'Benjamin Netanyahu addresses 2018 AIPAC Confab', Haaretz.Com, https://www.haaretz.com/israel-news/full-text-benjamin-netanyahu-addresses-2018-aipac-confab-1.5883524 (accessed 16 August 2020)

279 Nicholas Davis, 'What is the Fourth Industrial Revolution?', World Economic Forum, 19 January 2016, https://www.weforum.org/agenda/2016/01/what-is-the-fourth-industrial-revolution/ (accessed 10 February 2021)

280 Payce Madden, 'Figures of the week: Africa's preparedness for the Fourth Industrial Revolution', Brookings, 11 March 2020, https://www.brookings.edu/blog/africa-in-focus/2020/03/11/figures-of-the-week-africas-preparedness-for-the-fourth-industrial-revolution/ (accessed 18 August 2020)

281 Jack Ma, 'If we do not change the way we teach, thirty years from now we will be in trouble', https://www.youtube.com/watch?v=pQCF3PtAaSg (accessed 22 September 2020)

282 Nick Wingfield, 'As Amazon pushes forward with robots, workers find new roles', *The New York Times*, 10 September 2017, https://www.nytimes.com/2017/09/10/technology/amazon-robots-workers.html (accessed 13 September 2020)

283 James Manyika and Kevin Sneader, 'AI, automation, and the future of work: Ten things to solve for (Tech4Good)', McKinsey, 1 July, 2018, https://www.mckinsey.com/featured-insights/future-of-work/ai-automation-and-the-future-of-work-ten-things-to-solve-for (accessed 13 September 2020)

284 World Bank Tweet (14 August 2020)

285 'Baraka Obama's Feb. 5 Speech', *New York Times*, 5 February 2008, https://www.nytimes.com/2008/02/05/us/politics/05text-obama.html (accessed 15 May 2021)

286 'September 2009 Barack Obama speech to a joint session of Congress', *Wikipedia*, https://en.wikipedia.org/wiki/September_2009_Barack_Obama_speech_to_a_joint_session_of_Congress#cite_note-khabrein1-6 (accessed 15 May 2021)

Index